D1029746

ETHICS

ETHICS
A Short Introduction

Robert G. Olson
The Brooklyn Center
Long Island University

Random House, New York

First Edition
98765432
Copyright © 1978 by Random House, Inc.

Library of Congress Cataloging in Publication Data
Olson, Robert Goodwin, 1924–
    Ethics.

    Bibliography: p.
    Includes index.
    1. Ethics. I. Title.
BJ1025.045   170   77–24713

ISBN 0–394–32033–6

Manufactured in the United States of America

Text design by Deborah H. Payne

PREFACE

Ethics: A Short Introduction was written expressly for beginning college students and presupposes no background in philosophy. I have tried to cover as clearly and briefly as possible not only the basic issues in traditional ethics but also related issues in social philosophy.

The combination of brevity and readability makes the book suitable for many different uses. It could, for example, be part of the reading assignment for an introductory course in philosophy, for a course in political and social philosophy, or for an interdisciplinary course in human values. The book was originally conceived, however, as a background text for use in ethics courses. Particularly, it is intended for ethics courses that are taught from an anthology or other group of readings dealing with specific substantive questions such as capital punishment, civil disobedience, racism, women's liberation, suicide, abortion, sexual freedom, and drug use.

Like many instructors today, I find the newer books dealing with concrete moral issues a welcome corrective to the older texts with their heavy emphasis on historical and metaethical issues. The newer texts do, however, pose a problem of their own. Almost all differences of opinion on specific moral questions reflect differences of opinion on more basic questions. For example, controversy about the rights of blacks, of women, and of other disadvantaged groups normally involves differences of opinion about the nature of individual rights, of justice, and of freedom. Similarly, controversy with regard to abortion, suicide, and sexual freedom often turns on differing views with respect to the role of religion in determining what is right or wrong. But the format of the newer texts does not permit a systematic treatment of these underlying questions. *Ethics: A Short Introduction* was designed to provide the required background and perspective.

The final draft of this book owes much to the advice and criticism of many friends and colleagues, as well as to several anonymous readers for the publisher. I should like especially to thank Albert Blumberg, William J. Earle, Paul Edwards, Eli Hirsch, Bruce Nissen, and Karsten J. Struhl.

R.G.O.

CONTENTS

CHAPTER 5 Religion and Morality   119

CHAPTER 6 Right Conduct   143

ETHICS

The Good Life

For many people the word "ethics" suggests primarily a moral code, or a body of rules of right conduct. And, of course, this is one of the common meanings of the term. As a branch of philosophy, however, ethics has to do with much more than standards of right conduct. For example, moral philosophers also deal with personal happiness—which is the subject matter of the present chapter—and with the good society—which is the subject matter of the chapter to follow. Moreover, the concept of right conduct seems to presuppose the concept of the good society, insofar as for most people one of the crucial tests of any moral code is its tendency to promote the good society. And the concept of a good society, in turn, seems to presuppose the concept of personal happiness, since for most people a good society must by definition promote individual well-being.

It would be wrong, however, to suppose that personal happiness, or individual well-being, is a pivotal concept on which all ethical issues turn. The central issues in moral philosophy are related to one another in a tight web of complex interrelationships. If, for example, our concept of personal happiness tends to shape our concept of the good society, our concept of the good society also tends to shape our concept of personal happiness. It could hardly be otherwise. As we shall see in later chapters, human beings are by nature social animals. Even their physical existence depends on membership in a human community. The fact that this book begins with a discussion of individual well-being, therefore, is merely a matter of expository convenience.

The concept of personal happiness, or individual well-being, concerns what are customarily called *intrinsic goods*—things that are valued for their own sake and that contribute directly to making life worthwhile. Intrinsic goods are contrasted with *instrumental goods*—things that are valued for their consequences and that contribute to the good life only indirectly. For example, good health and good music are intrinsic goods. We appreciate them in and of themselves. They enter into the good life directly as parts of a whole. Painful surgical operations and tedious hours of practice on a musical instrument, on the other hand, are instrumental goods, since they are not valued in and of themselves and do not as such form parts of the good life. Their value is that of instruments, means, or tools, which are appreciated only indirectly, as conditions for the achievement of intrinsic goods.

The conceptual distinction between intrinsic goods and instrumental goods is simple and straightforward. But many actual goods are valued both for their own sakes and for their consequences, both as ends and as means. In fact, almost any instrumental good that is not positively painful or otherwise disagreeable will in time come to be appreciated for itself and hence become an intrinsic as well as an instrumental good. For example, money is in the first instance an instrumental good. Young children when they first learn what money is appreciate it exclusively as an instrumental good. And for adults, unless they are misers, money continues to be primarily an instrumental good. Yet there are few adults to whom a large bank balance or a big sum of cash at hand does not give a direct and immediate satisfaction. Conversely, most intrinsic goods are also instrumental goods. Health, for example, is appreciated for its own sake, but it is no less appreciated for the many enjoyable activities it makes possible. Even happiness, which by definition is an intrinsic good, tends also to be an instrumental good. For a happy person often radiates happiness, one person's happiness being a source of happiness for others.

Concrete intrinsic goods are surprisingly varied: good health, good music, good food, Picassos, chess games, love affairs, friendships, interesting work, beautiful sunsets, foreign travel, mystical experiences, and countless other things. Moreover, what is a concrete good for one person may not be a concrete good for another; it may in fact be an evil for the second person. For example, some people like vigorous exercise while others detest it. Some people like big families. Others prefer small families or no families at all. These individual differences give meaning to a remark of British playwright George

Bernard Shaw: "Do not do unto others as you would have others do unto you. Their tastes may be different."

Nevertheless, most traditional moral philosophers have tended to define happiness in terms of some one thing. Typically, they have made two major contentions:

1. Most of the things human beings regard as concrete goods have a single common characteristic in terms of which happiness ought to be defined. According to some traditional philosophers, for example, almost all things valued as concrete goods are alike in that they involve pleasure. Thus, although some persons prefer large families and others small families, the reason for this difference is simply that some persons find pleasure in large families whereas others find pleasure in small families. It follows that although from one point of view small families and large families are different and even opposing goods, from another point of view small families and large families are alike in that they both provide pleasure to human beings. Shaw's remark, therefore, cannot be accepted without qualification. Properly interpreted, the saying "Do unto others as you would have others do unto you" does not mean that if a friend is sick and needs something to read I should give the friend a detective story because if I were sick and needed reading matter I would want a detective story. A more appropriate interpretation would be that if a friend is sick and in need of something to read I should give the friend a book the friend will enjoy just as I would like a book I would enjoy in similar circumstances.

2. Traditional philosophers recognized, of course, that at least a few of the things ordinarily regarded as concrete goods do not possess that single characteristic, or feature, in terms of which they believed happiness ought to be defined. Thus, their second major contention is that these things are not genuine goods but are regarded as goods only out of ignorance or misunderstanding. For example, many a small child has mistakenly supposed that pleasure would result from contact with fire.

The features of concrete goods that make them good are called *good-making characteristics*. The view that happiness consists in an abundance of concrete goods with one and only one good-making characteristic will be called the *classical view of happiness*. Various versions of this classical view are discussed in this chapter. The chapter closes with a discussion of a more modern view of happiness, according to which there is more than one good-making characteristic.

Pleasure

Those philosophers who define happiness as pleasure, arguing that pleasure is the one and only good-making characteristic, are called *hedonists*. Hedonism has been championed by two major philosophical schools. One, called Epicureanism, was founded by the Greek philosopher Epicurus in the fourth century B.C. and continued to thrive throughout the first few centuries of the Christian era. The second, called utilitarianism, was founded by the English philosopher Jeremy Bentham in the late eighteenth century and has flourished under the inspiration of the nineteenth-century English philosopher John Stuart Mill up to the present day. As we shall see later, the utilitarians are best known for a doctrine that has no necessary connection with hedonism, but in their own eyes hedonism was an integral part of their philosophy.

None of the hedonists has given us a clear definition of "pleasure." This is unfortunate, since the term is ambiguous. As ordinarily used, it has a wide and a narrow usage. Sometimes when we say that a concrete good is a pleasure, we are using the term broadly and mean simply that the good has some good-making characteristic, something that makes it desirable or satisfying. When at other times we say that a concrete good is a pleasure, we are using the term narrowly and mean that it gives us the kind of gratification that normally accompanies the fulfillment of physical appetites for food, drink, and sex.

Interpreted according to either of these two common usages, hedonism is not a very satisfactory doctrine. If the term "pleasure" is used broadly, the doctrine is true but empty and uninteresting. If the good, or happy, life consists of many concrete goods with one satisfying, desirable, or good-making characteristic, then what we need is a specific description of that good-making characteristic. But if "pleasurable" means exactly the same as "good-making," then "pleasurable" cannot be used to describe, or specify, the nature of the good-making characteristic. On the other hand, if the word "pleasure" is used narrowly to refer to the kind of gratification that accompanies the fulfillment of physical appetites, then it is almost certainly false that all genuine concrete goods provide pleasure. For there are many goods, especially those of a mental or spiritual character—clear conscience, creative endeavors, good conversation, and so forth—that appear to be qualitatively quite different from physical gratifications.

The ambiguity of the term "pleasure" is reflected in an exchange between Epicurus and one of his critics. When the latter claimed that hedonists underestimated the worth of human beings and reduced them to the level of pigs, Epicurus retorted that it was the critic who underestimated humankind by assuming that human beings are capable of only those pleasures experienced by pigs.

Although all of the classical hedonists explicitly disavowed the notion of pleasure as mere physical gratification, the narrow usage of the term "pleasure" persists. In ordinary language even the terms "hedonistic" and "epicurean" are used to describe persons who live primarily for physical gratifications. And, as already noted, the hedonists failed to explain clearly how their use of the word "pleasure" differed either from the narrow popular usage or from the broader usage described above.

The Relative Merits of Concrete Goods

Although hedonism suffers seriously from the absence of a suitable definition of "pleasure," the hedonists have made many important contributions to moral philosophy. One of the most interesting and useful contributions comes from Jeremy Bentham, who proposed a set of criteria, or considerations, that ought to be kept in mind whenever we must decide which of two proposed concrete goods is the greater, or more satisfying. This set of criteria is called the *hedonistic calculus,* or the *calculus of pleasures.* The use of the terms "hedonistic" and "pleasures" is misleading, since the criteria apply to the evaluation of almost any concrete good, whether or not it is appropriately called a "pleasure." The use of the term "calculus" is also misleading, since it suggests a method of evaluating the relative merits of concrete goods with mathematical exactitude, although Bentham made no such exaggerated claims for his calculus.

What follows is a simplified and somewhat modified account of Bentham's calculus. This account consists of five criteria that we ought to consider when choosing between concrete goods or deciding which of two proposed concrete goods is the greater.

The first of the five criteria is *intensity.* Other things being equal, the more intense good is preferable to, or greater than, the less intense. In some cases it is difficult to determine which of two possible goods is the more intense. In many cases, however, there can be no reasonable doubt. For example, the pleasure of orgasm is surely more intense than the pleasure of thumb-twiddling.

The second criterion is *duration.* Other things being equal, the longer a concrete good lasts, the greater it is. Thus, according to this criterion, an evening of good theater is superior to the pleasure of orgasm, a month of agreeable tranquillity preferable to a moment of intense excitement. Sometimes this criterion, too, is difficult to apply, but generally it is even easier to apply than the criterion of intensity. It is important, however, to give due weight to the phrase "other things being equal." Although it is obvious that an evening of theater lasts longer than an orgasm and is superior *in this respect,* it is by no means obvious that a long experience of moderate intensity is, all things considered, superior to a short experience of great intensity. But, clearly, we could not make wise or informed choices if we did not consider duration along with intensity and the other criteria yet to be discussed.

The third criterion is *propinquity,* by which Bentham meant nearness in time. The point of this criterion is aptly expressed in the saying, "A bird in the hand is worth two in the bush." Because all possible future goods pose some degree of uncertainty, present goods have an edge over future goods when all else is equal. Again, however, attention must be called to the phrase "when all else is equal." A small child, if given the choice between a lollipop now and a million dollars at age twenty-one, would probably choose the lollipop now. But, clearly, the mere fact that the lollipop is a nearer, or more immediate, good does not justify the child's choice. What the classical moral philosophers called "prudence," and what we today often call "postponement of gratification," is essential to the good life.

The fourth criterion is *fecundity,* by which Bentham meant the tendency of some goods to create additional goods in the future. For example, the pleasure of listening to good music is usually fecund. The more good music one listens to, the more likely one is to train one's ear and to increase one's capacity for enjoying good music in the future.

The last, and probably the most important, of the criteria is *purity.* The purity of a pleasure is measured by the degree of pain or unpleasantness it may involve, whether directly or indirectly. Accordingly, the pleasure of the sexual masochist—a pleasure that by definition involves pain—is impure. Similarly, the pleasure of playing a musical instrument well insofar as this ability is the result of difficult and unpleasant drill is impure. And so is the pleasure of heavy drinking when it leads to accidents, fights, hangovers, and other forms of unpleasantness. Obviously, pure pleasures should be preferred to impure pleasures, all else being equal. Totally pure pleasures, however, are rare; it is a truism that most of the goods available to human beings can be had only at a price. We cannot, therefore, reject a good simply because it is impure. But, unfortunately, the term "impure" suggests outright condemnation. To avoid this suggestion, the term "mixed good" is sometimes used in place of "impure good."

Living for the Present

As already noted, the classical philosophical hedonists rejected the definition of "pleasure" as physical gratification. They also rejected a heavy emphasis on propinquity as a criterion in the selection of goods. Epicurus took a dim view of the physical pleasures and urged a far greater degree of moderation in sex, drink, and food than most Christian moralists. (For Epicurus the highest human values were friendship and good conversation.) He also acknowledged the importance of a prudent regard for one's future well-being. Nonetheless, hedonism commonly suggests not only a life dedicated to physical pleasures but also a life dedicated to the pleasures of the moment without regard to the future. In the popular mind hedonism is summed up in the old Roman motto: "Eat, drink, and be merry; for tomorrow we die." Since this moral outlook is not without its supporters today, a few observations about this view may be helpful.

On the one hand, it is undeniable that propinquity is a legitimate criterion for the evaluation of goods. It is also undeniable that the less stable one's situation is—that is, the harder it is to make trustworthy plans for the future—the more legitimate it is to prefer present pleasures to possible future pleasures. And since the twentieth century is clearly a time of often unpredictable social change, it is understandable and proper that present generations should live less for the future and more for the present than did many previous generations.

On the other hand, as almost all of the classical moral philosophers rightly insisted, human beings have a strong and irrational tendency to overvalue present gratifications and to undervalue future goods. In each of us there is something of the child who prefers a lollipop today to a million dollars at age twenty-one. This tendency is the result of two universal human weaknesses. The first weakness is the inability to imagine, or picture, future goods as concretely as present goods. The pleasures near at hand are vivid and make a strong appeal. Distant pleasures do not so insistently command our attention. The second weakness is the unwillingness to make the efforts or sacrifices that so often constitute the price of future goods. We too often prefer moderately pleasant evenings of television now to the solid future good of professional success, only because the latter requires some present sacrifice. Reason tells us that the sacrifice is worthwhile or even essential, but we lazily reject the advice of reason and allow ourselves to be lured by the call of immediate pleasure. The ability to defer gratification is, according to many psychologists, one of the best measures of maturity. It is also one of the most difficult, though rewarding, of human achievements.

There is still another problem with the idea of living for the present. Most people who favor this idea tend to think of the present as rich, lively, and exciting. They also tend to dismiss the past—which, they say, is no more—and the future—which, they say, still is not—as impoverished or lesser realities.

But it is clear that this particular concept of the present is unacceptable. First, the idea of the present is very elastic. The present may mean this minute, this hour, this day, this month, this year, this century, this millennium, the Christian era, and so forth. The length or "stretch" of the present depends on the context or perspective we adopt. Moreover, whatever stretch of time we take to be the present necessarily contains a bit of the past and a bit of the future. If it did not, it would not be a "stretch" of time. And if it were not a stretch of time, it would be nothing. Some philosophers even assert that the present is the most questionable aspect of time. The present, they say, is nothing but a kind of vanishing point where past and future intersect. Second, almost any "present moment" of time in human experience that counts as good reflects the past in memory and the future in hope. A present with no links to the past and no links to the future is rarely rich, lively, and exciting. Normally, it is empty, pale, and dull.

Of course, there are people whose past is so horrible that they choose to forget it and whose future is so grim that they prefer to ignore it. And, possibly, we cannot fault them for taking refuge in "the present," given their circumstances. But we must remember two things: (1) They can never wholly escape the past and the future, which are inescapable dimensions of human experience. (2) The relief they achieve by unburdening themselves of past and future is wholly unlike the robust and wholesome satisfactions of a happy person. It is rather a meager gratification of someone whose life has been irreparably damaged.

Life According to Nature

An important rival to hedonism in classical times was the position that happiness is achieved by living in conformity with nature. This view was proposed by the famous Greek philosopher Aristotle in the fourth century B.C. It entered Christian—especially Roman Catholic —moral philosophy when adopted by St. Thomas Aquinas in the thirteenth century. The contemporary use of the term "unnatural" to condemn certain sexual practices and certain methods of contraception has its roots in this view. So, too, does the contemporary tendency to use the term "natural" as a term of praise.

The chief difficulty with this position, as with hedonism, involves the meaning of the key term. Exactly what Aristotle and St. Thomas meant by the term "natural" is a matter of controversy among scholars, but before attempting to understand their meaning we shall examine a few common uses of the term that definitely do not apply.

One ordinary meaning is typical, average, or common, as when we say that it is only natural to be suspicious of strangers. But neither Aristotle nor St. Thomas meant to say that happiness is achieved by being an average person. In fact, Aristotle and St. Thomas both believed, as did most traditional philosophers, that relatively few persons are happy.

Another common meaning of "natural" not intended by Aristotle and St. Thomas is unreflective, nondeliberate, or spontaneous. For instance, in the song from the musical comedy *Annie Get Your Gun* the heroine explains her lapses from conventional sexual morality as a matter of "Doin' What Comes Natur'lly." For Aristotle and St. Thomas, however, as for most traditional philosophers, deliberation, or taking thought before acting, is strongly recommended.

Finally, there is a common use of "natural" in which the natural is contrasted with the artificial—that is, made by human beings—as in the distinction between natural and artificial pearls. This third common usage is related to the philosophical meaning intended by St.

Thomas. The Roman Catholic condemnation of "artificial" methods of contraception and approval of "natural" methods (such as withdrawal and the so-called rhythm method) presupposes this distinction. Yet this cannot be the primary meaning of "natural" for those who see happiness as a product of natural activities. Neither Aristotle nor St. Thomas condemned the use of all artificial devices for the achievement of human ends. Plows, roads, and books—which are not condemned—are no less human creations than condemned contraceptive devices.

What, then, did Aristotle and St. Thomas mean when they urged us to seek happiness through conformity with nature? It seems that two primary meanings of "natural" were intended.

One of these meanings rests on a doctrine known as *teleology*. This doctrine exists in two versions. According to the first version all natural, as opposed to artificial, objects have an inner purpose or in-dwelling goal. When one is acting naturally, therefore, one's behavior shows a proper respect for these inner purposes, or goals. For example, St. Thomas maintained that the purpose of sexual organs is reproduction. Consequently, he said, one is behaving "naturally" when one engages in sexual intercourse for the purpose of procreating, but "unnaturally" when the manner or circumstances of sexual behavior make procreation impossible.

Most contemporary philosophers, however, reject this version of teleology together with the corresponding use of the word "natural." They argue that purposes, or ends, are primarily associated with the desires or intentions of conscious beings. Sexual organs, since they are not conscious, have purposes only in the way that plows, roads, and books do. They are means to ends, or instrumental goods, whose value is wholly relative to and determined by the purposes of conscious beings. And since human beings engage in sexual intercourse to obtain pleasure and to express love as well as to procreate, it makes as much sense to say that the purpose of sexual organs is pleasure or the expression of love as to say that their purpose is procreation.

It has, of course, been argued that God gave us sexual organs for the purpose of procreation and that the proper end of sexual behavior ought to be determined in relation to God's purposes or intentions, not ours. But if this is what is meant by saying that intercourse is natural only when people engage in it for the purpose of procreation, the use of the term "natural" seems to be misleading. After all, God is usually considered a supernatural, not a natural, being. Would it not, therefore, be clearer and simpler to say that the use of sexual organs for procreation is divinely approved, whereas their use for other purposes is divinely disapproved?

The second version of teleology holds that Nature, or the totality of what exists, has an overall order, plan, or design. Accordingly, the purpose of the sexual organs, for example, is to be understood not by reference to some purpose of those organs themselves—or even to divine or human purposes—but rather by reference to the plan of Nature as a whole. This version of teleology avoids some of the difficulties of the first version, but it does not solve the central problem. It merely displaces the problem. For those who find it odd to attribute purposes to sexual organs find it equally odd to attribute purposes to Nature. The critics argue that when we attribute a design, or purpose, to Nature, we are doing one of two things. (1.) We may be presupposing that Nature is the creation of God, in which case the so-called design of Nature is, properly speaking, the design of God. (2.) We may be making an unconscious or uncritical analogy between humankind and Nature, in which case we are guilty of *anthropomorphism,* the unwarranted attribution of human traits to the nonhuman. Nature as such is nonhuman and nonpersonal. It, therefore, has no consciousness and, consequently, no intentions, purposes, goals, ends, or designs.

The second meaning of "natural" apparently intended by Aristotle and St. Thomas rests on a doctrine sometimes called *essentialism.* According to this doctrine everything has some inner "essence," or "nature," that makes it and all other things of its kind what they are and distinguishes this class, or species, of things from all other things. For example, Aristotle said that the nature, or essence, of Socrates is rationality, since rationality is common to all human beings and differentiates them from other animal species. Thus, another term for "nature" or "essence" is "specific difference."

In this view the properties of an individual or species are either *essential* or *contingent.* Socrates, who happened to be snub-nosed, could have been long-nosed without altering his essence, or nature, without ceasing to be what he was. Being snub-nosed is, therefore, merely a contingent property. But if Socrates had ceased to be rational, he would have ceased to be what he was. His essence, or nature, would have been violated. He would have lost his species identification. Rationality, therefore, is an essential property.

In accordance with the doctrine of essentialism, human beings behave naturally when they act so as to develop to the full their specific difference, or essential rationality. Human beings behave unnaturally when they frustrate the full realization of their specific nature.

But why should happiness consist in behavior that accords with our specific nature, or in the exercise of our capacities as rational beings? By itself essentialism does not answer this question. The answer lies in essentialism plus certain other Aristotelian doctrines.

One of these doctrines is that rationality is a property human beings share with God and that through the proper exercise of reason we participate in divinity. But many persons question Aristotle's assumption that participation in the divine nature is necessarily a good-making characteristic for the human species. The difference between God and human beings may be such that a good-making characteristic for God is not a good-making characteristic for us.

Another doctrine linking Aristotle's essentialism with the view that happiness consists in activity in accordance with our nature is known as the *doctrine of fixed species.* According to this doctrine the individual members of a species are finite and mortal whereas the species themselves are eternal and unchanging. It is, therefore, only through species identification that the individual can hope for immortality.

A third relevant Aristotelian doctrine is that animal species fall into a hierarchy of value and that the human species is at the top of the hierarchy. Behavior in conformity with our human nature, therefore, has a special kind of nobility.

These last two doctrines have suffered heavy blows as a result of evolutionary theory. If evolutionary theory is correct, then no animal species is necessarily immortal. Each comes into existence at some point in the evolutionary process and may someday be extinct, as are the dinosaurs. Similarly, if evolutionary theory is true, then the human species is the "highest" only in the weak sense that humankind is the latest and the most complex species yet to emerge. And, clearly, this evolutionary view of humankind does not give us any reason to suppose that a property distinguishing human beings as a species is necessarily a good-making characteristic. The effect of a successful evolutionary process is the survival of a species, not the happiness of its individual members.

A still more radical challenge to essentialism comes from a large group of contemporary philosophers who argue that Aristotle completely misunderstood the concept of essential properties. For Aristotle essential properties are given, or determined, by Nature and discovered by us. When we say that the essence, or nature, of humankind is rationality, we are saying something about humankind. For most contemporary philosophers, however, essential properties are defining properties, and what we define are words, not things. Thus, when we say that humankind is essentially rational, we are not talking about humankind. Instead, we are talking about the word "humankind." An analogy may clarify this point. The essence of bachelorhood is the state of being unmarried. When we say this, however, we are not saying something about, or adding to our knowledge of, the state of being a bachelor. Rather, we are saying something about the word "bachelor"—namely, that the word ought not to be applied to someone unless he is unmarried. Similarly, if we say that the essence of humankind is rationality, we are not saying something about human beings. Rather, we are saying that we think it would be improper or unwise to use the word "human" to refer to a being who is nonrational.

This modern challenge can be stated somewhat differently. Although Aristotle did not seem to be consistently aware of it, there are many traits that distinguish human beings from other animal species. Humankind is the only animal who barters, or trades, one thing for another. The Scottish economist Adam Smith said that he had never seen two dogs get up on their hind legs and exchange bones. Humankind is the only animal that makes and uses tools. Humankind is the only animal who makes and keeps promises. Humankind is the only animal who knows that death is inevitable. And so forth. But none of these traits comes stamped with a label saying "I am the essence of humankind." Instead—collectively or individually, consciously or unconsciously—human beings select one or more of these specific differences as defining properties of the word "humankind," prohibiting the use of that word to refer to beings that lack these traits. The question of essences, or natures, is thus primarily one of deciding the properties a thing must have in order for it to be designated by a certain term. Only indirectly, if at all, is it a question of discovering some truth about a previously identified class of individuals.

Self-Realization

Historically, the view that happiness consists in self-realization has been closely allied with the view discussed in the preceding section, since self-realization is best interpreted to mean the fulfillment of one's "nature." It, therefore, shares all the difficulties associated with the notion of "nature." In fact, these difficulties are even greater for most self-realization theorists. For self-realization theorists typically hold that the nature of the individual consists not in the properties the individual shares with other members of its species, but rather in a set of properties that makes that individual unique, there being as many different natures and modes of self-realization as there are individual human beings. And it is generally agreed that when an individual's nature is conceived not in terms of species indentification but rather as something peculiar to the individual, the concept becomes even less clear. Moreover, the classical theories of happiness as self-realization have usually been advanced as parts of much larger philosophical systems that today have few supporters. In what follows, therefore, we shall deal exclusively with two popular ideas that seem to be a legacy of the classical theories.

One of these popular ideas is that each of us realizes selfhood and achieves happiness by exercising whatever individual potentialities, abilities, or talents we happen to possess. There is more than a grain of truth in this view. A person with keen artistic sensitivities is unlikely to be happy as a file clerk. All of us have potentialities that must be fulfilled if we are to grow satisfactorily and enjoy even a moderate measure of happiness. Moreover, it is probably safe to say that many of these potentialities are not universal. Many represent individual temperamental biases or peculiarities.

It is clear, however, that each of us has far more potentialities than could possibly be realized in a single lifetime. Most people, for example, have the capacity to pursue successfully many different vocations or careers, but few people are able actually to realize more than a few of these potentialities. In fact, many of our potentialities contradict one another. No one, for example, could become a well-known public figure and simultaneously an ordinary, private citizen. Thus, although happiness requires the fulfillment of some of our potentialities, it also requires the ability to accept the fact that some sides of our "nature" must remain unfulfilled. Persons bent on realizing *all* of their potentialities would be constantly frustrated.

The second popular version of the self-realization theory holds that we realize ourselves and achieve happiness by fulfilling not our potentialities, abilities, or talents, but our conscious desires, whatever those desires happen to be. The great and obvious difficulty with this view is that many people desire things that are bad for them. Drug addicts, alcoholics, and victims of other compulsions are engaged in self-destruction rather than self-fulfillment. An infant who desires to touch a flame discovers that realization of the desire brings not the anticipated pleasure, but sharp pain.

To save the theory it is necessary to qualify the term "desire." Self-realization and happiness must be viewed not as the result of fulfilling whatever we happen consciously to desire but rather as the result of fulfilling "genuine," "real," or "true" desires. Although it cannot be denied that the drug addict and the alcoholic do in some sense desire the drug or alcohol they pursue, it can be argued that in a deeper sense they do not desire it. As a rule, their attitudes toward drugs or liquor are ambivalent. How else could one explain their frequent efforts to free themselves from their addictions or habits? Similarly, an infant who consciously desires to touch a flame does so expecting some sort of gratification; and it is not farfetched to say that the infant "genuinely," "really," or "truly" desires the anticipated pleasure rather than the act of putting the hand in the flame. But if happiness is to be defined successfully in terms of the fulfillment of "genuine" desires, as opposed to consciously experienced desires, then we need some clear basis for the distinction between the two kinds of desires. Unfortunately, attempts to find such a basis have not been notably successful.

Even if this problem could be solved, there remains another and still more basic problem. If happiness consists in the fulfillment of desires, how can we explain the fact that many persons who have "everything," whose every whim is instantly gratified, are unhappy. And how can we explain why many persons who, to all appearances, are exceptionally happy are ardently pursuing goals, often unachievable in their lifetimes? In order to deal with these questions more adequately a view must be examined that at first appears to be the opposite of the one under discussion—namely, the view that happiness can be achieved only through the renunciation of desire.

Renunciation

The doctrine that happiness consists not in the fulfillment of desire but rather in the renunciation of desire is very old. In the Western world it was advanced by the Stoics, who were contemporaries of the Epicureans, and it has been evident in many strands of Christian thought up to the present day. In the Eastern world this doctrine is even older and has found even wider acceptance, especially in Hindu and Buddhist thinking. The exact meaning of *nirvana*—a term frequently used in both Hindu and Buddhist literature—is a matter of dispute. It is clear, however, that "nirvana" is roughly equivalent to "salvation" and that the chief characteristic of the state of nirvana is absence of craving, or release from desire. Interestingly enough, the state of nirvana is often associated with selflessness, the antithesis of the goal of self-fulfillment advocated by the self-realization theorists.

Those who recommend a state of "desirelessness" usually stress two points. First, they argue that desire by its very nature implies unhappiness. As Aristotle's teacher, Plato, had his own teacher, Socrates, point out in one of Plato's most intriguing and influential dialogues, *The Symposium,* a perfectly happy being such as God has no desires. We desire only what we lack, and God has everything that he could possibly want. In this respect those who advocate renunciation and those who advocate fulfillment of desire agree. It is precisely because of their common belief that to desire is to be unhappy that the one group recommends fulfillment of desire whereas the other recommends renunciation of desire. It is also because of this common belief that the renunciationists must show that the fulfillment or realization of desire does not bring happiness.

To prove this point two related arguments are advanced. One is that the satisfactions accompanying the achievement of desired goals do not compensate for the unhappiness involved in the pursuit of those goals. All goods associated with desire fulfillment are highly impure, or mixed. The other argument is that the satisfactions experienced upon the fulfillment of desires are necessarily short-lived, inevitably lead to boredom, and thereby tend to force us back into the "round" or "wheel" of desire. In other words, desire is like an itch. And the fulfillment of desire is like the sensation we experience when we scratch the itch—a sick and short-lived satisfaction that only exacerbates the itch and leaves us worse off than we were before.

Although the renunciationists have overstated their case, it does seem to be true that if happiness consists in fulfillment of desire, life for most people will be primarily the pursuit of happiness and only incidentally or episodically happiness itself. Most pleasures are fleeting, and those that last have a tendency in time to pall. Moreover, the attempt to satisfy many desires can easily lead to morbid habits—drug addiction, alcoholism, insatiable drives for money, power, and sex.

The view that happiness consists in fulfillment of desire is similar to that expressed by the last line in the fable, "They lived happily ever after." Both are naïve and unrealistic.

The real difficulty for renunciationists lies in the contention, shared by their opponents, that a desiring being is unhappy simply because desire implies lack, or the pursuit of unfulfilled goals. Of course, the pursuit of goals can be frustrating and disagreeable. But it need not be and often is not. For some students, especially those with little academic aptitude or those who have acute financial problems, the pursuit of a college degree may be a heavy "grind." But for others, especially those with pronounced academic abilities and ample time to devote to their studies, the pursuit of a college degree is usually a highly satisfying experience. The idea that if we pursue goals whose realization lies in the future, we do so for the sake of future satisfactions is at best a half truth. We also pursue future goals in order to enhance the quality of our present experience. As a matter of fact, one of the greatest sources of human distress is the absence of well-defined goals in terms of which we can organize and orient present experience. Conversely, one of the most important ingredients of happiness is a well-defined set of goals that gives meaning and purpose to one's present experience. Compared to the satisfaction conferred by this sense of meaning and purpose, the satisfaction involved in the fulfillment of desire is of minor importance. And it is for this reason that persons who dedicate themselves to distant goals that cannot even be achieved in their lifetimes are often happier than those who pursue and successfully achieve many short-range goals.

Before abandoning our discussion of happiness as a matter of renouncing desire, it is advisable to look at the issue from another point of view, one often adopted by the Stoics. According to this perspective we advance toward happiness by closing the gap between what we want and what we have, between the way we want things to be and the way things are. Conceivably, the gap could be closed in either of two ways: (a) by changing our environment or altering the circumstances of our lives, thereby permitting the realization of our desires; or (b) by renouncing our desires and learning to accept things as they are. As we have already seen, the Stoics advocated the second way rather than the first. They believed that the satisfactions accompanying the achievement of our desires are highly impure and that the pursuit of these satisfactions leads to a wearisome "round of desire." The Stoics had, however, another reason for renouncing the effort to fulfill our desires. For the Stoics, as for many classical philosophers, happiness is something that lies within the individual's control, something that does not depend upon accident or good fortune. But, they said, the fulfillment of our desires always depends on external circumstances beyond our control, whereas the renunciation of our desires, which are parts of the self, depends only on our will. Thus, it is always preferable to renounce a desire rather than to seek its fulfillment.

The weakness in this argument lies in the claim that because desires are internal parts of the self they are more easily subject to the individual's control than external circumstances. Many desires are extremely resistant to voluntary control. Ask any heavy smoker or drinker. At the same time all of us, regardless of how modest our intelligence and talents, have successfully manipulated at least some aspects of our environment. The one-sided Stoic emphasis on renunciation is, therefore, difficult to justify. Sometimes it is best to modify our desires, reconciling ourselves to things as they are. At other times it is best to pursue our goals by actively restructuring our environment. An old religious formula sums it up well: "May God give me the strength to change what I can, the patience to endure what I cannot change, and the wisdom to know the difference." Using a secular and more technical vocabulary, the twentieth-century American pragmatist John Dewey has said that a good individual *adjustment* to (or satisfactory interaction with) the natural and social environment has two dimensions: *accommodation* and *adaptation*. A well-adjusted person accommodates to, or learns to accept, the disagreeable features of the environment that cannot be changed while, simultaneously, adapting, molding, or manipulating the features of the environment that can be changed. Intelligence is the means by which we determine which of these two techniques is appropriate in any given situation.

A Contemporary View

So far we have been discussing the classical view of happiness, according to which all genuine concrete goods possess a single good-making characteristic in terms of which happiness ought to be defined. As we said earlier, contemporary philosophers tend to reject this classical view—not merely the various versions of the classical view but the very concept of happiness as some one thing. Philosophers today have not, however, gone to the other extreme and adopted the notion that happiness is indefinable, that it consists in something wholly different for each individual. The contemporary view is rather that the concept of happiness is complex and that a proper definition of happiness has to include several different good-making characteristics. Concrete goods vary from one individual to another just as different individuals derive pleasure from different things. But the good-making characteristics are the same for everyone.

There is also general agreement today that the term "happiness" is inherently vague. Happiness is a matter of degree, and it is unreasonable to expect a definition of "happiness" that permits us to establish precisely to whom the term applies and to whom it does not apply. In all probability there will always be borderline cases—people who are not exactly happy but who are not unhappy either. The degree of happiness depends on the number of good-making characteristics present in an individual's life and the extent to which these characteristics are present. But nobody can say exactly how many must be present or in what degree for a person to be happy. Nor is precision of this kind necessary. The practical purpose of a definition of happiness is to clarify the directions in which we must move in order to achieve personal well-being, not to categorize people.

Beyond this point there is little general agreement among today's philosophers on the definition of happiness. But there is also little controversy, since only a few contemporary philosophers have even tried to formulate a concrete definition of happiness. The following definition, which lists five good-making characteristics, therefore, does not represent any substantial body of opinion.

Pleasure. Although there are few outright hedonists today, there are also few people who deny that pleasure, even narrowly defined, is one good-making characteristic, one element in the good life. Other things being equal, a life with many pleasures is better than a life with few pleasures.

Maximizing pleasure is not, however, so simple a matter as many amateur hedonists seem to think. First, as Bentham pointed out with his hedonistic calculus, the concept of a *greater* pleasure is highly complex. A pleasure may be greater in intensity but lesser in duration. A pleasure may be greater if we ignore factors such as propinquity, fecundity, or purity, but lesser if such factors are taken into account. Few of us, however, take all of these factors into account. As a matter of fact, most people are unaware that the greatness, or magnitude, of a pleasure has so many different dimensions.

Second, since most pleasures are mixed, or impure, we easily make two kinds of error. Sometimes, we mistakenly forgo a pleasure because we are unwilling to undergo the discipline or sacrifice required for its achievement. And, sometimes, we mistakenly insist upon a pleasure because we do not properly weigh disagreeable future consequences.

Third, most of us do not give sufficient credit to the measure of truth in the Stoic contention that the pursuit of pleasure generates sick desires that we would be better off without. For example, consider how the pleasure afforded by an occasional cigarette after a good meal or in a moment of tension can lead to a three-pack-a-day habit in which the only pleasure is the satisfaction of what amounts to a nervous itch.

There is still another problem in maximizing pleasure that has not been touched on so far. This problem is sometimes called "the paradox of pleasure": the fact that the deliberate and conscious pursuit of pleasure frequently inhibits the achievement of pleasure. According to some philosophers—especially those who define happiness as activity in accordance with nature—the deliberate and conscious pursuit of pleasure is always inhibiting and all genuine pleasures are by-products of activities pursued with other goals in mind. Although common experience does not seem to support this extreme view, experience does strongly suggest that we often do not experience an anticipated pleasure because of an overanxious desire to bring it about. And it does seem reasonable to suppose that the person who lives more or less exclusively for pleasure in the narrow sense of that term, equating happiness with a succession of physical or quasi-physical gratifications, achieves less pleasure than a person for whom pleasure occupies a less important place in the everyday, conscious scale of values.

Purposeful activity. As we saw earlier, a number of classical philosophers tended to see progress toward happiness as a matter of reducing the gap between what one has and what one wants. According to self-realization theorists that gap is best reduced by fulfilling one's desires. According to the Stoics the gap is best reduced by renouncing one's desires. It appears, however, that both groups are wrong, and wrong for the same reason. Purposeful activity, which presupposes a gap between the way things are and the way one wants them to be, is not a source of unhappiness but rather a condition of happiness. To have and to pursue goals is a major intrinsic good, an indispensable part of the good life. This is not to say that there is no such thing as frustration, that one cannot be unhappy because one pursues goals that are unrealizable or realizable only at too great a cost. The point is that the opposite of frustration is not happiness but boredom, tedium, or purposelessness. To enjoy the good life it is necessary to find some sort of balance between the opposing extremes of frustration and boredom. Purposeful activity, in other words, is an ingredient in the good life, but only on condition that the goals we pursue are neither so challenging as to leave us with a sense of frustration, defeat, and disappointment nor so petty as to leave us with a sense that life is empty, vain, and meaningless. For many people the sense of purpose is derived principally from their careers or work activities, but family-related projects and dedication to causes are also important sources of this ingredient in the good life.

It is not always easy to achieve the proper balance between boredom and frustration, to find activities that give life meaning and purpose without making life into a grim and hopeless battle. To achieve this desirable goal at least three things are required. First, there must be some understanding of one's temperamental peculiarities, for the threshold of frustration, or point at which frustration sets in, varies considerably from one individual to another. Some people need a degree of risk, challenge, and adventure that others find altogether intolerable. On the other hand, some persons are perfectly content to pursue goals that others regard as insignificant or even contemptible. No matter what one's temperamental bias, however, everyone must have some insight into one's temperamental bias to ward off the opposing threats of boredom and frustration.

Second, there must be a realistic appraisal of one's talents and abilities. Those who overestimate their capacities run the risk of frustration, whereas those who underestimate their capacities run the risk of failing to discover rewarding activities that give life a greater sense of purpose. As pointed out earlier, however, almost all human beings have far more capacities than they can reasonably expect to realize during the course of a lifetime, and the person who tries to realize all of them will be sorely frustrated.

Finally, to achieve a proper balance between boredom and frustration one must learn accurately to appraise the opportunities and possibilities offered by one's environment. If regard is paid only to a given individual's temperament and aptitudes, a medical career may be indicated above all others. But if in that individual's society there is a surplus of doctors or if there is little possibility of admission to a medical school, the wisest choice may be a different career. In the language of Dewey the well-adjusted person must be adept at accommodation as well as at adaptation.

Satisfying human relationships. Human beings are essentially social beings and cannot lead a recognizably human life apart from other members of their kind. Unlike other social animals such as bees and ants, however, human beings have a remarkable variety of relationships with others of their species. During the course of a lifetime the typical human being relates to others as family member, friend, co-worker, lover, fellow citizen, casual acquaintance, employer or employee, student or teacher, doctor or patient, leader or follower, and so on. Many of these relationships have a biological or economic basis and are intended to perpetuate the race or to serve the need for material well-being. Some are necessary conditions for purposeful activity. Others, however, are basically intrinsic goods that we value as a source of warmth, affection, and psychological security.

Not only are there many kinds of possible human relationships, there are also great differences in individual needs. For some people sexual relationships and romantic love have an overwhelming importance. For others family and parenthood are paramount. For still others close friendships or group associations are crucial. And so on. There is, therefore, no simple recipe for securing the intrinsic satisfactions that may accompany our relations with others. Satisfying human relations, like purposeful activities, are essential ingredients in the good life. But the concrete patterns of good human relationships, like the concrete patterns of purposeful activities, vary greatly. And in both cases success depends largely on the extent and accuracy of the individual's knowledge of self and social circumstances.

Sense of personal worth. Various factors contribute to the sense of our personal worth as human beings. Some people, for example, derive a sense of worth from the religious conviction that they have been made in the image and likeness of God, whereas others suffer in self-esteem because of the belief that they are miserable sinners who deserve eternal punishment in hell. (More will be said about this in Chapter Five.) A second factor for a number of people is their conception of themselves as moral beings. The eighteenth-century German philosopher Immanuel Kant, for example, believed that the greatest of all intrinsic goods for a human being is the sense of dignity experienced when conforming to the moral law. And no doubt many people have suffered grievously from moral guilt or bad conscience.

(This topic will be elaborated on in Chapter Four.) Third, the feeling of individual worth is often related to the possession of certain individual rights, or civil liberties, and to democratic institutions that enable people to participate actively in the political process. Surely, the absence of such political rights has often been suffered as an indignity. (We will discuss these points further in Chapter Three.)

It seems, however, that for most people the two most important factors shaping their self-image are purposeful activities and the respect of others with whom they are closely associated. People who have undertaken well-chosen projects enjoy a feeling of power and self-expansion as a result of the constructive use of their native talents. And people who are surrounded by friends, colleagues, and others who respect them almost always respect themselves. On the other hand, those who have no meaningful projects or who cannot count on the esteem of others are almost always troubled by feelings of insecurity or inferiority. Whatever the factors that shape an individual's self-evaluation may be, however, a positive self-image is an important part of the good life.

Physical well-being. Ordinarily, physical well-being is a condition of the successful experience of any of the four intrinsic goods thus far mentioned. It is also undeniably an intrinsic good, something valued in its own right without regard to the many good things it makes possible. This is so evident that there is little need to comment on this particular element of the good life. Since, however, those who enjoy physical well-being often take their good fortune for granted, it is perhaps appropriate to point out that throughout the twentieth century approximately half of the world's population has been seriously undernourished. If, therefore, this fifth criterion of well-being poses few theoretical problems, it does call our attention to one of the most serious political problems facing the community of nations. It also serves as a dramatic reminder of the extent to which personal well-being depends on favorable social circumstances.

Chapter 2

The Good Society

If one society provides more personal well-being to more people than a second, most of us would agree that the first is a better society. But what must a society be like in order to maximize personal well-being? What social conditions promote or impede the individual happiness of society's members? These questions form the subject matter of Chapter Two.

More specifically, in this chapter we shall discuss six social ideals, or goals—stability, harmony, social cohesion, justice, freedom, and material prosperity—that are widely believed to promote individual well-being. In Chapter Three we shall deal with problems relating to the kinds of political and economic institutions that best further these ideals.

Stability

Of all the animal species humankind is best able to adapt to unfamiliar circumstances. There are several reasons for our superior adaptability. First, although many other animal species have sensory equipment that we lack, none has developed so many and such refined senses as the human species, and none has so powerful a drive to explore the environment. As a consequence much more of the external world is available to us.

Second, in all animal species, what is perceived in the external world tends to act as a signal, or stimulus, triggering some sort of behavioral response. When a tendency to respond to an environmental stimulus with a certain type of behavior is inborn or unlearned, it is called an *instinct*. A familiar example of a human instinct is the blinking reflex—that is, the inborn and unlearned tendency to respond to the sudden appearance of any object near the eye by blinking. Our instinctual nature differs from that of other animals, however, in a very important respect: human instincts are usually much less rigid. Instincts like the blinking reflex in which a specific stimulus evokes a specific response are the exception rather than the rule among human beings. Among other animals, on the contrary, almost all instincts are highly specific. For example, consider the hunger instinct. Among most nonhuman animals there is an instinctual response to only a few foods. If for any reason the foods to which one of these species has been programmed to respond disappear, the species dies out. Human beings, on the other hand, are capable of responding to a wide variety of food stimuli. This greater plasticity of human instinct means that human beings have a greater possibility of altering their behavior to meet the challenge of changing circumstances.

Finally, human beings differ from other animals in that we have a superior intelligence that permits us to learn more from past experience and better to anticipate, or predict, the future. Just as our greater sensory awareness and drive to know extends our world horizontally, so our intelligence extends our world vertically into the past and into the future. And although there is no generally agreed upon definition of intelligence, there is widespread agreement that its principal role in the evolutionary process is to help the species adapt to changing circumstances by anticipating them.

In sum, other animals—whose awareness of the world is restricted, whose instincts are fixed, and whose intelligence is limited—do not ordinarily foresee adverse environmental changes and are usually helpless when they occur. Human beings, however, can often foresee and adjust to such changes.

In view of our superior adaptability it might be thought that stability does not rank high as a social ideal. Since we can better adapt to changing circumstances, they seem to be less threatening to us. But this inference is erroneous. The very factors that make us adaptable also generate a need for stability. Indeed, it is no exaggeration to say that some measure of stability is the most basic of all human needs.

The fact that we live in a larger world means a greater awareness of dangers and outside threats. Since, for example, other animals do not know that they can be destroyed by any number of natural catastrophes, they do not live in fear of these catastrophes. Human beings often do. And the fact that our behavior is less rigidly instinctual means that we must reflect and choose and are therefore prey to all of the anxieties, doubts, and hesitations that accompany reflection and choice. Moreover, intelligence itself requires a reasonably stable environment in order to function well. Under completely unstable, or anarchic, social conditions nothing is predictable and intelligent planning is impossible. For people to adapt intelligently to unfamiliar and unforeseen social changes there must be a relatively stable background of order. If, for example, an individual unexpectedly loses a job and needs other employment, coping intelligently with this situation requires a basically stable overall pattern of employment opportunities. If the kinds of jobs available and the qualifications for these jobs are subject to constant and unforeseeable change, the job seeker cannot plan intelligently and must rely on luck.

Of course, stability by itself does not make a good society. A good society must satisfy other social ideals. Moreover, the ideal of stability can often conflict with these other social ideals. For example, a runaway slave in the United States before Abolition could confidently expect to be severely treated if apprehended. But the stability represented by the maintenance of the slave system conflicted with justice. Similarly, material betterment often requires technological advance, which generates insecurity for workers whose skills may become obsolete.

One should not, however, attach too much importance to the fact that the ideal of stability sometimes conflicts with other social ideals. The conflict of social ideals is a familiar theme, and almost any ideal can conflict with almost any other. Stability is not unique in this respect. Nonetheless, out of regard for the fact that stability when broadly defined often conflicts with other social goals, the term "social stability" is often defined more narrowly. Stability becomes the maintenance of major institutions such as those that constitute the broad framework of a country's economic system and that vitally affect the interests of many people. Relatively minor institutions such as styles of dress or advertising techniques are left out of account. And many people limit the concept of social stability even further, linking it almost exclusively to the stability of decision-making procedures. Stability and order are found in the process of change itself rather than in the maintenance of the status quo. Persons who point with pride to the fact that the United States has survived over two hundred years under the same constitution usually have this kind of stability in mind.

It is often said that political conservatives tend to rank stability as a social ideal higher than those to the left of the political spectrum. Indeed, liberals and radicals of the left are often accused of anarchist leanings. There are two reasons for this accusation. First, in a conflict between stability and other social ideals, especially justice, liberals and left radicals often choose the alternative ideals. It must not be thought, however, that every effort to achieve greater social justice or other social goals necessarily destabilizes society. For just as social ideals may conflict, so they may reinforce one another. There can be little question that justice, for instance, tends to stabilize society. Certainly, long-standing and uncorrected injustices have been a major cause of most revolutions and other major social disorders.

Second, the left is by definition more sympathetic to social change than the right, and many people see all social change as inherently destabilizing. Change in and of itself, however, does not make a society unstable. For example, if society could look forward confidently to a steady increase in material prosperity or steady progress toward social justice, it would not for this reason be less stable. Instability follows not from change itself but from unpredictable change. Predictable change is wholly compatible with stability.

Moreover, most of the changes advocated by the left are advocated because they are believed to promote greater stability. Measures designed to increase job security, for example, are expected to stabilize workers' lives and to facilitate long-range planning. Even when those to the left advocate steps resulting in true instability, as opposed to mere change or orderly progress, these steps are usually considered part of the price that must be paid for greater future stability. For example, one reason revolutionary socialists are willing to tolerate the genuine instability of a transitional revolutionary situation is that they believe the ultimate result will be a more stable society. Capitalism, they argue, is inherently unstable and anarchic. The absence of overall planning has made its history a succession of unpredicted and unpredictable ups and downs. Only a socialist society, they say, can be truly stable.

Social Harmony

As noted in Chapter One, humankind is one of the most thoroughly social of all animal species. As also noted, human sociality is more complex than that of the lower social animals. There is, however, an even more crucial difference between human sociality and that of the lower animals. In a beehive or an ant colony individual behavior that benefits the community is determined almost wholly by instinct or biological programming. In human societies, on the other hand, almost all socially desirable behavior must be socially induced. For example, without a substantial measure of mutual trust fostered by practices such as telling the truth and keeping promises human communities could not survive. But human beings have no inborn or unlearned tendency to tell the truth or to keep promises. If society does not somehow teach or otherwise encourage the individual to tell the truth and to keep promises, the individual never learns. In many cases—for example, bravery on the battlefield and restraint in sexual behavior—socially desirable behavior actually runs counter to unlearned, biologically determined behavior patterns.

Human beings are often said to be *gregarious,* to have a natural tendency to seek out the company of other human beings. This is undoubtedly true. It is a part of what is meant in calling humankind a social animal. At the same time, however, human beings are often extremely suspicious and fearful of one another. And this is an additional fact that makes the nature and degree of social influence on individual behavior a matter of such overwhelming importance. To some extent our fear and distrust of one another results from our being in general more fear-prone than other animal species insofar as we live in a larger world and are aware of dangers to which other animals are blind. But there are two more specific reasons for the human individual's distrust of others of the same species.

First, the human individual is exceptionally dependent on other members of the human race. The period from birth until adulthood, during which individuals in almost all animal species are heavily dependent on others, is far longer among human beings than among other social animals. Furthermore, the individual human being is not only materially dependent on others—this material dependency is common to all social animals—but also psychologically dependent in a variety of ways unknown among lower animals. Lower animals, for example, do not worry about becoming involved in scandals. Nor do they make vows of lifelong fidelity or worry that such vows will be broken. Our extreme dependency on other human beings means that we are almost constantly concerned that others may become indifferent to us or withdraw their support.

Second, for reasons still poorly understood human beings are far more aggressive in their dealings with one another than are members of the lower animal species. With the possible exception of ants and rats humankind is the only animal to make war. As a matter of fact, any form of aggressive behavior resulting in the death of a member of one's own species is rarer among the lower animals than among human beings. Lower animals do, of course, frequently kill members of different species, and among members of the same species competitive combat for food, territory, or sexual object is common. But predatory behavior aimed at members of other species has as its human counterpart animal slaughter for food and must be sharply distinguished from *intraspecies aggression,* or aggression among individuals within the same species. Furthermore, as just indicated, intraspecies aggression among the lower animals rarely leads to death. As a rule, the victorious animal in a contest with another of the same species is content with a ritual sign of defeat from the victim and almost invariably spares the victim's life. Among human beings death from other forms of homicide is as common as death from military combat.

There is another way of putting the points just stated. The dangers that beset any animal species are of four kinds: (1) the weakness of the body, disease, and physical pain, (2) natural catastrophes such as floods, earthquakes, and tornadoes, (3) the aggression of other animal species, and (4) the aggression or noncooperation of other members of one's own species. Of these dangers the first three tend to predominate among the lower animals. Among the human species, as most of us may confirm by consulting our own experience, the fourth predominates.

It should be carefully noted that the threats human beings pose to one another occupy this uniquely important place in the catalogue of dangers despite the fact that human beings have always been social animals and have always been subject to social controls. One shudders to think, therefore, what life would be like in the absence of all forms of social control, in what the seventeenth-century English philosopher Thomas Hobbes called a *state of nature,* as opposed to humankind's actual social state. In the words of Hobbes a state of nature would be a "state of war" in which everyone is pitted against everyone else and in which the life of all would be "solitary, poor, nasty, brutish, and short." Of course, the phrase "state of war" must be understood figuratively, since conventional war presupposes a degree of social organization impossible in a state of nature. Hobbes' essential point is simply that a state of nature implies a measure of conflict and insecurity that utterly frustrates the quest for human well-being.

How, then, does the community get individuals to behave in socially desirable ways? How does society manage to weaken the attitudes of distrust, fear, indifference, and hostility that coexist with our gregariousness and threaten to undermine successful social living? How does it manage to channel instinctual energies in socially useful directions? How does it prevent disintegration into a state of nature where unhindered individual self-seeking produces a war of each against all from which no one emerges a victor? In short, how does society manage to reconcile different individual interests so as to produce social harmony?

Two basic strategies are used to secure social harmony. The first consists in structuring, or designing, the environment so that socially desirable behavior is rewarded and socially undesirable behavior punished. In other words, society institutes a set of *external sanctions*— environmental rewards or penalties—that make it advantageous for individuals to pursue socially desirable goals that would otherwise not be in their best interests and to refrain from the pursuit of socially undesirable goals that would otherwise be in their best interests. Sanctions that penalize individuals are called *negative sanctions;* sanctions that reward them, *positive sanctions.*

Society employs a variety of external sanctions. Some—for example, terms of imprisonment, called "penal sanctions"—are legal; others are nonlegal. Some are physical—for example, spankings, floggings, and capital punishment. Some are material, or economic—for example, pay raises, fines, and tax exemptions for charitable gifts Others are moral—that is, they involve praise and blame or other means by which human beings show approval or disapproval, respect or contempt, for one another.

The second basic strategy that society uses to harmonize conflicting individual interests consists in shaping the character or personality of the individual. Psychologists often refer to this process as *socialization.* It is also appropriately called *moral education,* provided that the term "education" is used broadly enough to include not only formal schooling but any other social influence on the development of individual character. In Chapter Four, which is devoted to an analysis of desirable character traits, we shall discuss in some detail what character traits society has an interest in cultivating and how it attempts to do so. Certain of these traits, however, are so crucial to social harmony that we must say a few brief words about them here.

One part of the socializing process is the development of *rationality,* by which we mean a set of dispositions or habits that permit us (a) to increase our knowledge and (b) to extend the range of behavior in which proper deliberation and due regard for our best all-round, long-range interests play a proper role. The importance of rationality in promoting social harmony is not always sufficiently appreciated. Yet much antisocial behavior is due not to evil intent but rather to irrational willfulness, shortsightedness, and ignorance. Also, the effectiveness of the external social sanctions in promoting harmony depends on individual rationality. For few of the rewards and penalties society uses to encourage or discourage behavior come into play immediately. Most are delayed, and some are delayed considerably. For example, it takes many years to develop a reputation as a person of integrity. It is, therefore, essential that individuals learn to look to the future, to weigh the consequences of their behavior, and to forgo immediate gratifications of an antisocial character in favor of long-term social rewards.

Another part of the socializing process consists in the development of two important character traits that expose individuals to what are often called *internal moral sanctions.* One of these character traits may be called *conscientiousness.* Conscientious persons have a sense of duty or moral conscience. When they act in ways they believe to be antisocial or morally wrong, they experience a loss of self-esteem or a feeling of unworthiness. They suffer from, or are punished by, a bad conscience or a feeling of guilt. On the other hand, when conscientious persons behave well despite temptation, they tend to experience feelings of pride and self-respect. They are rewarded with a good conscience. The second of these character traits is called *benevolence,* or *altruism.* Benevolent, or altruistic, persons experience some form of personal disturbance or pain when confronted with the unhappiness or suffering of others. The suffering of others causes them to suffer. At the same time, when confronted with the happiness of other human beings, benevolent persons feel a sense of personal well-being, pleasure, or delight. The happiness of others causes them to be happy.

Obviously, conscientiousness and benevolence when strongly developed in many of a society's members greatly increase the chances of social harmony. Even in a very imperfect society the internal moral sanctions have a substantial role to play. A society that had to rely on external sanctions alone to keep the murder rate within reasonable bounds would be at most one step above the state of nature. Surely, no one would care to live in a society whose members were so lacking in concern for others and so unscrupulous that only the fear of imprisonment, material penalties, or other external sanctions restrained them from murdering one another.

Social Cohesion

In this section we shall be dealing with *social cohesion,* or *group solidarity,* by which we mean the tendency of individuals to identify with their society, to feel that they are to society as parts to the whole Social cohesion is closely related to patriotism, or love of country. And the development of ties that bind people into large social units such as nations is part of the process of socialization, an additional means by which society secures greater social harmony. We are treating the topic of social cohesion separately only because it poses special problems.

It has often been suggested that the basis of social cohesion is material, or economic: the need of individuals to cooperate in order to ensure physical well-being. But this cannot be the whole story. First, economic interests appear to divide people—along class and regional lines, for example—as much as they unite them. In fact, many people feel that one of the chief values of social cohesion is precisely its usefulness in getting groups with conflicting economic interests to work together. Second, economic relations are usually cold, calculated, and impersonal. They, therefore, fail to explain the peculiar emotional quality of our involvement with our group or country. There are few, if any, symbols that command such strong feeling as a flag. And, typically, individuals react to the desecration of the flag not as they would to an economic loss but rather as they would to a personal insult.

A much better explanation of most instances of social cohesion is in terms of general allegiance to social tradition. As a rule, the more cohesive a society is, the more general and profound its dedication to the beliefs, values, and institutions forged by preceding generations. And although it is conceivable that an individual would feel profound allegiance to a social tradition without believing that tradition to be superior to the traditions of other countries, in practice this rarely happens. Historically, social cohesion based on a commitment to social tradition has gone hand in hand with an *ingroup-outgroup mentality,* or a tendency to exalt one's own society while dismissing other societies not merely as different but also as inferior. In primitive cultures and even in some highly developed cultures such as classical Greece the ingroup-outgroup feeling was often so intense that other peoples were barely regarded as human. The word "barbarian" was originally a Greek word that meant simply non-Greek. Still in the twentieth century social cohesion often carries with it an irrational sense of the superiority of one's own society and an unreasoning contempt for other social groups. Significantly, social cohesion is usually strongest in times of war, when mindless chauvinism and arrogant hostility toward the enemy is most encouraged.

Although few people question the historical fact that allegiance to tradition and an invidious ingroup-outgroup mentality have played a primary role in fostering social cohesion, many doubt the desirability of this state of affairs. First, in a world as interdependent as ours and with such an advanced technology wars are far more destructive than in the past. It is, therefore, crucial that we avoid international hostilities based on an exaggerated sense of group superiority and unreasoning contempt for outgroups. Second, the irrational feeling of ingroup superiority inhibits national self-criticism and self-improvement. People in whom this feeling is strong tend to see all criticism of country, however justified, as unpatriotic or subversive. Finally, although the drive to bolster one's sense of self-worth through group identification is nearly universal, it is of questionable morality. Almost everybody agrees that a positive self-image should be based on personal achievement, not mere group identification. Like white supremacists and male chauvinists, national chauvinists all too often build themselves up at the expense of outgroups and take unwarranted personal credit for the alleged achievements of others in their ingroup.

Some people, although aware of the disadvantages of building social cohesion on a basis of blind devotion to tradition and contempt for other cultures, have argued that no other effective way of building social solidarity exists. It seems, however, that this view is unnecessarily pessimistic.

First, a considerable degree of group cohesion may be achieved through a common commitment not to past traditions but to future goals. Analogies between individuals and groups should always be used cautiously. Nonetheless, just as individual well-being depends to a great degree on purposeful activity, so national well-being may depend on a common endeavor to achieve shared goals. A country moving in well-defined directions in accordance with a forward-looking national plan that mobilizes the energies of the citizenry could probably boast of at least as much social cohesion as a country drifting along in an atmosphere of smug self-satisfaction.

Second, social cohesion may be significantly fostered by political and social institutions that encourage broad participation in the decision-making processes that affect national life. Indeed, it seems to be difficult to participate actively in the decisions that affect the directions in which a group moves without identifying with that group.

Closely related to the question of social cohesion at the national level is the question of ethnic identity within a culturally diverse country such as the United States. Is ethnic identity or social cohesion a desirable thing among such groups as American blacks, American Jews, Polish Americans, Italian Americans, German Americans, and so forth. According to one common view in the United States, known as *integrationism,* a strong sense of ethnic identity should be discouraged. The United States is essentially and by rights should continue to be a "melting pot." The various minority ethnic groups should be encouraged to integrate into the mainstream culture. According to a second view, often called *cultural pluralism,* the sense of ethnic identity should be actively encouraged.

Those who favor integration usually stress the dangers of the ingroup-outgroup mentality, insisting that the cultivation of ethnic identity creates tensions and animosities that are undesirable in themselves and that also threaten social cohesion at the national level. Those who favor cultural pluralism, on the other hand, often argue that a variety of ethnic groups adds color and vitality to national life and need be no more divisive than religious differences have become in the twentieth century. For even if one grants that social cohesion at the national level requires a widespread commitment to common ideals, there is no reason that tolerance, mutual forbearance, and a commitment to diversity should not count among those overarching ideals that contribute to the basic sense of national cohesion.

Distributive Justice

We speak about justice in two different contexts. Sometimes the question is to decide how someone who has broken the law or the moral code should be punished. This kind of justice is known as *punitive justice,* or *corrective justice,* and will be discussed in Chapter Six. Other times the question of justice is that of deciding how the goods or resources available within a given society ought to be distributed among its members. Justice in this second sense is known as *distributive justice.* Distributive justice alone will concern us in this chapter.

Since the eighteenth century claims for greater social justice have been closely allied to claims for greater equality. In fact, for many people today "justice" and "equality" are practically synonyms. According to the Declaration of Independence by the American colonies in 1776, all men are "created equal." Therefore, it has been inferred, all men have an equal claim to the goods of this earth. These goods should be distributed according to the principle of *strict equality.* For example, if there are ten persons and ten bushels of potatoes, each person should receive one bushel. Although at first blush the principle of strict equality seems to be sound, almost nobody would accept it after serious consideration. Suppose, for example, that one of the persons among whom the ten bushels are to be distributed is a two-hundred-pound laborer, another a one-hundred-pound desk worker, and a third a new-born infant. Suppose, again, that five of the ten persons had worked hard to produce the potatoes while the other five had refused to work at this or any other productive process. Suppose, finally, that all ten persons contribute to the productive process, but that through a mutually agreed on arrangement whereby the more productive workers are given a somewhat greater share of the product output could be greatly increased and everybody would get considerably more than a single bushel. In none of these cases would we be inclined to favor strict equality.

In order to get around the difficulties with the principle of strict equality the principle of *equality of opportunity* has often been proposed in its place. According to this amended principle of equality justice does not require that everyone receive an equal share of society's resources. Rather, everyone is entitled as a matter of justice to be able to compete for goods on equal terms with everyone else.

Accordingly, more productive persons may justly be given a greater share of the product, but only if they do not enjoy opportunities or advantages in the competitive struggle that are denied to competitors.

Despite its plausibility the principle of equality of opportunity does not fare significantly better than the principle of strict equality. First, there are so many natural inequalities among human beings that it is rarely possible for people to compete on equal terms. The Declaration of Independence notwithstanding, human beings are born unequal in many crucial respects. Some are born strong and healthy, others weak, sickly, or physically handicapped. Some are geniuses, others mentally retarded. Some are gifted with extraordinary special talents, others have very limited talents. And so forth. There are few competitive struggles, therefore, in which natural inequalities do not figure, in which none of the competitors enjoys advantages denied to the others. Second, as we shall see more fully later, the achievement of socially desired goals often requires that those whom Nature has favored be given greater opportunities than those who are less gifted. The quality of medical care would not be high if everyone were given an equal opportunity to enroll in medical school, nor would the level of achievement in baseball be high if everyone were given an equal opportunity to play on professional teams.

Thus, many philosophers have abandoned the attempt to define justice in terms of equality and have instead adopted what they consider a more promising approach. According to this approach, justice is defined formally in more or less the following terms: If any individual or group is given preferential treatment, there must be some relevant difference between the favored and the unfavored parties that justifies preferential treatment for the former. Thus, if because of what society does or fails to do, males have a greater share in society's goods, including the opportunities it makes available, there must be some difference between males and females that justifies the discriminatory treatment. Of course, this definition of justice, often called *the principle of justice*, does not take us far. It leaves us with the problem of deciding what kinds of differences among human beings justify different treatment. But it does provide a general framework for constructive dialogue.

Moreover, it is generally agreed that at least three kinds of differences among human beings do justify discriminatory treatment. The first of these is *need*. For example, parents are often justified in spending more money on a sick or handicapped child than on a healthy child. Similarly, schools and teachers are often justified in devoting more of their resources—time, money, teaching aids, and so on—to slow students than to average students. In this connection it should be noted that by distributing goods on the basis of need one does more to promote equality than by distributing goods on the basis of strict equality. For the major effect of distribution according to need is correction of natural and social inequalities. Special educational opportunities for the slow student, for example, compensate the student for Nature's unequal, or "unjust," distribution of intelligence.

The second relevant difference justifying discriminatory treatment is called *desert,* or *merit.* Although this basis for discriminatory treatment is at least as widely recognized and as often invoked as that of need, the meaning of the terms "desert" and "merit" is much less clear. For instance, most institutions of higher education admit some candidates and deny admission to others on the grounds that some are more deserving, or meritorious, than others. But it is rarely clear exactly what this means. For most of us the terms "merit" and "desert" suggest a confusing cluster of ideas.

One of these ideas is that of natural skill or ability. In the case of schools this is often said to be measured by tests of intelligence or academic aptitude. But it is difficult to see why anyone deserves favored treatment because of skills or abilities that have been inherited. It is generally recognized that people should be rewarded only for what they have done, not for what they have passively acquired. We may admire those who possess superior intelligence, physical strength, musical aptitude, and so forth, but we do not feel that they deserve a reward merely for being blessed with these gifts of nature. On the contrary, most of us feel that those whom Nature has favored, far from deserving a special reward, have a special social obligation. The principle of *noblesse oblige*—according to which those born to high social rank have special duties to society—has a counterpart in the principle that those favored by Nature have special social duties.

Another notion associated with "desert," or "merit," is that of past achievement. In the case of schools past achievement would ordinarily be measured by past academic records, especially grades or other evaluations of past performance. Reward for achievement is a more acceptable notion than reward for native skill or ability. But there are similar difficulties here. Superior achievement may be partially due to superior individual merit, but achievements are almost never entirely due to individual merit. In fact, merit often has little, or nothing, to do with them. First, a high level of achievement is often due to inborn talents or abilities, which as we have just seen do not in themselves deserve reward. Second, superior achievement is often due to social advantages, especially a favorable home environment in one's early years and the benefits of a high socio-economic status. And, of course, we are no more responsible for our upbringing or the socio-economic level into which we are born than we are for our hereditary endowment.

It would seem, therefore, that when we invoke desert, or merit, as a basis for preferential treatment what we really have in mind—or should have in mind—is the amount of effort or sacrifice that the preferred party has made. And, indeed, in clear-cut cases of merit a greater effort or sacrifice has always been made by the favored individuals. For example, if two persons are doing some type of disagreeable work, the one who puts in the greater number of hours, or sacrifices more time to the job, deserves a greater reward. Similarly, if two persons of equal physical strength and in the same state of health are engaged in the same simple physical task—let us say, carrying bricks—the one who expends more physical energy and carries more bricks deserves a greater reward.

If desert, or merit, is not more widely and immediately seen as a matter of greater effort or sacrifice, this may be attributed to three things. First, because the noun "justice" has no simple verbal equivalent, we often use the verbs "to merit" and "to deserve" instead of cumbersome phrases such as "to be entitled to as a matter of justice," thereby creating a confusion between the broader concept of justice itself and the narrower concept of merit, or desert. To avoid this confusion some philosophers have introduced the term "to justicize," but this term is not generally used even by philosophers. Second, effort or sacrifice is often difficult to measure directly, and for practical reasons we are frequently obliged to accept achievement as its most satisfactory measure. Finally, although superior native endowment does not in itself entitle anyone to greater opportunities or rewards, it is often in the interest of society to encourage the development of superior native talents. And we have a tendency to justify discriminatory treatment oversimply and incorrectly—in terms of superior talents themselves rather than in terms of the social values that discriminatory treatment based on natural gifts promotes. This brings us to the third generally recognized criterion of justice—social utility.

To say that favored treatment for one party at the expense of a second can be justified by *social utility* is to say (a) that the unequal treatment of the parties directly involved affects the welfare of some third party or parties and (b) that, given these third-party interests, the unequal treatment tends to promote the greatest possible well-being for all concerned. Consider, for example, admission to medical schools. If justice to the applicants were the only concern of medical schools, need and effort or sacrifice would be the only proper consider-ations. The natural abilities and past achievements of the candidates —except insofar as past achievement is a rough measure of effort— would have to be ignored. But medical schools have a social responsi-bility. They are expected to train people to provide good medical care to the general population. And it would be obviously unjust, or unfair, to the general population to ignore the applicants' natural abilities and past achievements, since these are of major importance in estimating the quality of their performance as future physicians.

Consider another example, which illustrates not only the impor-tance of social utility as a criterion of justice but also the ease with which this criterion becomes confused with the criterion of desert, or merit. College instructors are often asked to change a student's grade because the student has special needs or has made a special effort. Sometimes, if the needs are urgent or the effort has been truly excep-tional, instructors accede to these requests. It is generally agreed, however, that the grade a student "merits," or "deserves," depends primarily on the student's performance, or achievement. For the pri-mary social purpose of grading is to enable graduate schools and future employers better to predict how well a student will do in a particular program or job, and this purpose would be defeated if grades were based on need or effort rather than on performance. Unfortunately, the verbs "to merit" and "to deserve" are ambiguous, as we already noted. And since we have the term "social utility," which much more clearly explains the rationale of grading practices, we are well advised not to let the ambiguities of these verbs affect our use of the noun forms "merit" and "desert."

In sum, then, there are three types of differences among individuals that are generally agreed to justify preferential treatment: (1) greater need, (2) greater desert, or merit, interpreted to mean greater effort or sacrifice, and (3) social utility.

There is a question, however, as to how these criteria are related to one another and which ought to prevail when they conflict. The utilitarians Jeremy Bentham and John Stuart Mill, mentioned in the last chapter as supporters of hedonism, are better known for the doctrine of utilitarianism. According to utilitarianism an act is right if and only if it promotes the greatest happiness of the greatest number. An act of preferential treatment, therefore, must always be justified in the last analysis by the criterion of social utility. The criteria of need and merit are subordinate and in the event of conflict must give way to the criterion of social utility.

Indeed, according to the utilitarians, the criteria of need and merit owe whatever standing they have to the criterion of utility and must themselves be justified in terms of utility. If, other things being equal, we make a practice of giving preferential treatment to the needy, we do so because we thereby contribute to the greatest happiness of the greatest number. First, as Bentham pointed out, we must acknowledge the principle of *diminishing utility,* according to which the more one has of any good the less likely one is to benefit by an additional amount of that good. Clearly, extra food gives greater satisfaction to the hungry than to the well-fed, and an extra hundred dollars means more to a poorly paid worker than to a millionaire. Second, by distributing goods according to need, we allay the anxiety or insecurity of all those who, though not presently in need, fear that they too may at some future time be in need.

Similarly, if, other things being equal, we reward people for special efforts or sacrifices, we do so because we believe that important social benefits follow when people are encouraged to strive hard for certain ends. Efforts or sacrifices that serve no useful social purpose or that damage other human beings—for example, those that produce skilled pickpockets—do not deserve, or merit, reward.

Many persons today, however, find the utilitarian approach to distributive justice unsatisfactory. We shall see why when we examine utilitarianism more fully in Chapter Six.

One additional point regarding the question of distributive justice should be considered here. Some people have advanced a fourth criterion of justice: the individual's right to a share of the community's wealth equal to the *contribution* the individual has made in producing that wealth.

Often those who advocate this criterion also hold to the *labor theory of value,* according to which any commodity has a value that is determined by the amount of labor expended to produce it. Proponents of this theory tend to use it and the corresponding criterion of contribution to brand certain groups or classes as parasites who live off the labor of others. For example, St. Thomas Aquinas condemned moneylending on the grounds that moneylenders get a return on their money—thus a share of social wealth—without earning it. No productive labor is required to get a signature on a promissory note or to accept payment on money lent. Similarly, Karl Marx argued that capitalists *exploit* workers by paying them less than the value of what they produce and pocketing what remains, thus living off what Marx called *surplus value.*

The notion that those who contribute to a nation's store of wealth should be rewarded according to the size of their contribution is deeply rooted in our thinking, and the basic thrust of this idea is widely accepted. Nevertheless, many thinkers have rejected this fourth criterion on the grounds that it is unnecessary. They claim that ultimately the value of an individual's contribution to the community's well-being must be measured entirely in terms of the individual's merit and the social utility of the contribution. And, indeed, attempts to discover additional independent measures—for example, the Marxist attempt to equate the value of the output of labor with the number of hours of labor required to produce it—have been widely and vigorously criticized by non-Marxists.

Freedom

Historically, one of the most important meanings of a "free society" is the absence of colonial status or foreign domination. In many countries today this kind of freedom is a major social goal. As we will be using the term here, however, a "free society" is one that provides a relatively great measure of individual freedom to its members, just as a good society is one that fosters the well-being of its members. Freedom in the first sense is not, of course, an unimportant matter, it simply falls outside the scope of this book.

In order to discuss the social conditions that promote freedom it is necessary to analyze the concept of freedom, since its complexity is often insufficiently appreciated. As ordinarily used, the term "freedom" stands for two distinguishable things. One of these we shall call *freedom from restraint,* although it could also be called "freedom of achievement." Freedom from restraint is concerned with our ability to do what we want or choose to do without having to pay an excessive price or suffering from undue negative sanctions. A society that is substantially free in this respect is one in which its members have reasonable prospects of achieving the goals they set for themselves, in which the level of frustration encountered by individuals and groups as they pursue their chosen goals is relatively low. The second kind of freedom we shall call *freedom of choice*. Freedom of choice has to do with the number of options, or possible courses of action, society makes available to its members and the extent to which individual choices are informed and rational. We shall discuss each of these two kinds of freedom in turn.

Freedom from restraint—or the individual's ability to pursue chosen goals without excessive frustration—is obviously an important social goal. In an absolutely ideal, or utopian, society all of us would be able to do everything we wanted to do without paying any price whatsoever, without so much as a slight inconvenience. But, of course, absolute freedom of this sort is an unrealizable ideal. In the foreseeable future there will undoubtedly be people of bad character who want to do things that are hurtful to others, such as robbing or murdering, and who will have to be restrained for the good of others. There will also, of course, be persons whose understanding of their own needs is so limited that they must be restrained for their own good—for example, the very young, the mentally retarded, and the insane.

Moreover—and this is a point of far greater importance—even mature persons of good character and sound mind must be subjected to constant social restraints of various kinds in order to resolve fairly *conflicts of interests,* or situations in which the wants of at least one party will have to be frustrated if the wants of other parties are to be realized. For example, the desire of many smokers to indulge their habit whenever and wherever they wish is incompatible with the desire of many nonsmokers for smoke-free air. And it is difficult to see how a conflict like this could be resolved fairly without the use of social restraints enforced by negative sanctions—for example, obliging smokers to sit in segregated areas in airplanes, trains, public waiting rooms, and so on.

Given the pervasiveness of conflicts of interest, the old saying "One person's freedom ends where another person's freedom begins" expresses an important and undeniable truth. This is why we do not say that freedom from restraint consists in doing whatever one wants but rather in doing what one wants without paying an excessive price, or without undue frustration. Substantial restraints on individual behavior are an unavoidable part of social living. And in the case of certain acts—such as murder—society is not only permitted but obligated to frustrate the agent as much as possible and to exact a heavy price after the act.

The fact that substantial social restrictions on individual behavior are indispensable does not mean, however, that society cannot or should not attempt to increase individual freedom from restraint. There are several different ways in which individual freedom from restraint may be increased without undermining the foundations of communal living or doing serious damage to other social ideals.

First, every society would profit from institutionalized procedures whereby those who favor any given social restraint are continually challenged to produce well-reasoned and well-documented justifications. History offers numerous examples of restrictions on individual behavior that not only fail to serve the public interest but actually impede the achievement of the social goals they are supposed to serve.

Second, freedom from restraint can be increased by using less oppressive but equally effective restraints in place of unnecessarily severe restraints. Clearly, if a five-year prison term were an effective sanction for a certain crime, a ten-year term would be a needless limitation on individual freedom.

Particularly worthy of note here is the effect on freedom of substituting moral sanctions for physical, economic, or penal sanctions. As a rule, the person who has been well socialized and who refrains from antisocial behavior because of a conscientious regard for moral rules or an altruistic concern for the welfare of others finds these internal moral restraints less oppressive than external sanctions. Because they are internalized, they represent aspects of the agent's personality and are not experienced as outside repression. To the extent that the individual identifies with the community the external moral restraints are also experienced as less oppressive. There is an obvious difference between bowing to the will of a community because one counts oneself a full-fledged member and accepting a restriction on one's behavior simply to avoid imprisonment, financial loss, or some other nonmoral sanction.

One should not, however, jump to the conclusion that moral restraints never pose a danger to individual freedom or that they should be exempt from the kind of constant critical scrutiny that was just recommended for all social restraints. On the contrary! Almost everybody agrees today that the stern Puritan conscience that tormented people for minor offenses severely and unnecessarily curtailed individual freedom. And there can be no question of the oppressive nature of many external moral sanctions reflecting mere popular prejudice rather than reasoned consideration of the public good.

Finally, freedom from restraint may be increased by placing a heavier reliance on positive rather than negative sanctions to encourage socially desirable behavior. For example, to the extent that workers are motivated by negative sanctions—such as abrupt dismissals, deferred promotions, and salary losses—their freedom is threatened. They feel frustrated and hemmed in. When they are motivated by positive sanctions, however, such as material and moral rewards or intrinsic job satisfaction, their freedom from restraint is not diminished. In his well-known book *Walden Two* the contemporary American psychologist B. F. Skinner contended that in an ideal society positive sanctions—or, as Skinner says, positive reinforcements—for socially desirable behavior would be used exclusively.

We now turn to freedom of choice. We shall begin our discussion with an analysis of the concept of choice. Typically, a choice involves three elements. First, there is the chooser's perception of two or more possible courses of action. If we are trying to choose an occupation, for example, we will normally try to make some sort of mental catalogue of possible occupations. This mental catalogue will be called the *perceived range of options.* It will be contrasted with what we shall call the *objective range of options*—that is, the possible courses of action that are in fact open to the individual. This distinction is important because there is often a serious disparity between the perceived and the objective range of options. In choosing an occupation, for example, it is easy to overlook objective possibilities and just as easy to assume that a possibility exists when in fact it does not. Second, there is a process of deliberation in which the chooser weighs the relative advantages and disadvantages of the perceived options. This process of deliberation may be long or short. It may involve extensive inquiries and a diligent search for factual information, or it may involve no more than an attempt to get a certain feeling for the various options through the free play of the imagination. Finally, there is a realization or decision that one option is superior to the others and a resolution to act.

With this analysis of choice in mind, let us ask in what freedom of choice consists. Actually, it has two distinct aspects. One is largely external to the agent, the other largely internal. The external aspect is the objective range of options that society makes available. And the individual's freedom of choice is increased by increasing the number of options within that range. In primitive societies, for example, there was almost no freedom of choice with regard to occupation. As a rule, there was only one occupational role for men, and only one for women. By contrast in today's modern industrial societies there are literally thousands of distinct occupational roles and a corresponding gain in freedom of choice for the individual.

The internal aspect of free choice is the accuracy with which the individual's perceived range of options matches the objective range of options and the accuracy with which the individual assesses the relative merits of each option. Clearly, people are not free to choose an option if they do not even know that it exists. And, clearly, persons who can not correctly assess the relative merits and demerits of the available options will not be free to make informed and rational choices. Society, therefore, increases freedom of choice by making available the information necessary to assess accurately the number and relative standing of the available objective options and by educating individuals to make a rational use of the information provided.

Although freedom of choice is clearly distinguishable from freedom from restraint, freedom of choice is secondary in the sense that it is usually valued less in itself than as a condition of freedom from restraint. To confirm this one need only consider that although freedom of choice is increased by making more options available, not all options actually available increase freedom of choice. The person who is obliged to choose between being drawn and quartered or burned at the stake is not likely to thank his torturer for the "freedom" offered. Freedom is a good thing; having to make a choice like this is not. Objective options increase freedom of choice only if (a) their availability makes it possible to achieve goals that someone may actually desire and (b) their nonavailability is likely to be experienced as a restraint. For the person who has no desire to go to medical school the option of going has no direct personal value, and for the person who does want to go the absence of this option is experienced as a restraint.

Moreover, so far as freedom of choice is seen as a desirable social goal, it can be no more absolute than freedom from restraint. Just as the needs of social living make restraint on the individual's pursuit of personal goals inevitable, so social needs require restrictions on the objective range of options. Society must do what it can to eliminate the roles of thief and pickpocket from the available range of options.

And often it must exercise substantial control over the options that it does properly make available. If someone chooses to be a doctor, for example, it is right and proper that society determine the length and nature of the training. It is also right and proper that society exercise some form of supervision over the individual's eventual practice of medicine so as to ensure that patients receive good care.

The view of freedom of choice just presented appeals to common sense, and many philosophers are in sympathy with its general thrust. It has been sharply challenged, however, by a number of thinkers, who disagree on two major counts. First, the challengers argue that freedom of choice properly interpreted is not subject to any social influence. A choice made by a *socialized* agent from among a *socially* structured range of options is simply not a free choice. Freedom of choice is absolute and total, or it does not exist at all. Truly free choices are entirely self-caused, or self-determined. Second, the challengers argue that freedom of choice is not a secondary, or instrumental, value but rather an intrinsic value—and an intrinsic value of overriding importance that can be achieved only by sacrificing other important social goals such as stability, harmony, and freedom from restraint.

This second view of freedom of choice has been defended by a number of existentialists, especially by the nineteenth-century German philosopher Friedrich Nietzsche and the twentieth-century French philosopher Jean-Paul Sartre. But probably the most widely known version of this view is that of the nineteenth-century Russian novelist Feodor Dostoevsky as expressed in the famous *Legend of the Grand Inquisitor.* In this fable Dostoevsky paints a picture of a highly stable and harmonious society whose members have practically everything they want, in which freedom from restraint is almost total. This kind of society, he says, allows little or no freedom of choice and reduces the individual to the status of an ant in an ant hill or a bee in a beehive. Of necessity it is a regimented society in which benevolent tyrants oversee the fulfillment of everyone's basic biological needs and brainwash the masses into believing that they desire only those things their leaders want for them. On the other hand, Dostoevsky invites us to imagine a society where there is considerable freedom of choice. This society, he says, has little stability, little harmony, and little freedom from restraint. Of necessity a society marked by great individual freedom of choice is chaotic, unharmonious, and frustrating. For truly free individuals who choose for themselves without any social direction make wholly unpredictable and uncoordinated choices that defeat the pursuit of harmony and stability by would-be social planners. And in the absence of a basic framework of order and harmony individuals are inevitably frustrated in the pursuit of individual goals. This second kind of society is, however, redeemed by the individual dignity that accompanies free choice.

In other words, according to Dostoevsky humankind is confronted by a dilemma. In a society without freedom of choice individuals are regimented, brainwashed, and reduced to a nonhuman level. In a society with freedom of choice stability, harmony, and freedom to pursue one's goals without frustration must be sacrificed. But since free choice is what makes us distinctively human, it must be fought for and preserved at all costs. Freedom of choice must not be traded for security.

In rebuttal several points are made. First, the concept of absolute, or wholly self-determined, freedom of choice is rejected. Since human beings have always been social animals, they have always been subject to some form of socialization and have always lived in a social environment that prevents or penalizes the choice of certain options. If, therefore, free choice is so defined that it can exist only in a social vacuum, free choice does not exist at all.

Second, Dostoevsky's view seems to presuppose that every social control or influence restricts individual freedom. But this is said to be at best a dangerous half truth. It overlooks the fact that most social controls or influences liberate at least as much as they restrict. For example, laws against murder and robbery do restrict the action of would-be murderers and robbers, but they also increase the freedom of ordinary citizens who wish to live in safety. Similarly, compulsory education restricts the behavior of school children who prefer to play hookey, but it increases the freedom of these same children in their later adult pursuits. It is probably no exaggeration to say that the major purpose and most common justification of social restrictions is precisely their ultimately liberating effects. Thus, the crucial question bearing on freedom of choice is not whether the individual should or should not be subject to social influences but rather whether the social influences to which the individual is unavoidably subject tend in the final analysis and on the whole to increase or to diminish freedom.

Third, the contention that freedom of choice necessarily conflicts with stability, harmony, and freedom from restraint is rejected. Indeed, the claim is made that freedom of choice itself requires a high degree of these other social ideals. In the absence of a basic framework of stability, harmony, and freedom from restraint there can be no clearly defined options from among which we may choose and there can be no way of rationally evaluating the consequences of the options under consideration. This does not, of course, mean that freedom of choice cannot sometimes conflict with the other goals mentioned. For example, freedom of occupational choice could mean that large numbers of disagreeable but socially important jobs go undone. But the solution to such a conflict is not to reduce social controls. The solution is rather to make a more effective use of social controls. For example, ways might be found to provide greater rewards for the disagreeable tasks.

Fourth, criticism is made of the view that only a dictatorial or tyrannical government with a powerful propaganda apparatus can secure such values as stability, harmony, and freedom from restraint. For once the inevitability, the full extent, and the normal effects of social influences on individual choices are recognized, the task of predicting the patterns these choices will take and coordinating them in socially desirable ways is seen to be less formidable. It is only on the assumption that free choices are entirely self-caused, or self-determined, that we have any reason to expect that they will be so unpredictable and eccentric as to defeat democratic social planning. If, for example, everybody were to choose a career without regard to social circumstances, there would be no knowing what choices would be made. But the fact is that in all modern industrial societies job or career choices are made within a social framework, including (a) a certain range of job options or careers with a certain scale of rewards, (b) programs of job or career training, and (c) educational or guidance programs designed to help individuals choose from among (a) and (b). And since the patterns of free individual choices do predictably vary with alterations in these social circumstances, there is no reason to see free choice as inherently destabilizing or to suppose that any unwanted consequences of free choices can be counteracted only through physical coercion and mind control.

Finally, the view that wholly self-determined choices constitute an intrinsic good of overriding importance is rejected, as is the view that social influences on an individual's choices strip the individual of human dignity. Since absolute freedom of choice does not exist, it cannot be what makes us distinctively human, nor can it confer on us the kind of dignity that is lacking among ants and bees. The crucial difference between human beings and the lower social animals is that human beings have largely created their own social environment by the use of their intelligence, whereas the social environment of the ants and the bees is largely a product of blind evolutionary forces and pure instinct.

Accordingly, that which is distinctively human and confers true dignity on the individual is the exercise of rational powers. And whatever society does to encourage the individual to use those powers enhances rather than detracts from the individual's dignity. Once again, the serious social issue is seen not as the presence or absence of social influences on individual development but rather as the nature of those influences. Does a society educate and inform its members, or does it propagandize and censor? Does a society help its members to unfold and develop their powers of reasoning, or does it blunt and warp their minds? In other words, the claim is that those who rationally determine what objective options are available to them and properly deliberate on the respective merits of these options before choosing are making "their own choices" in the only intelligible sense that can be attributed to that expression. The mere fact that the range of options is socially determined and that the personalities of the deliberating agents show the influence of their social environments in no way detracts from their independence and dignity as free agents.

Of course, those who hold to the view of freedom of choice originally outlined in this section face two sets of extremely difficult and serious practical problems. First, who is to determine the social influences or controls to which individuals will be subject? Who is to decide what the available range of social options should be? Who is to decide what forms the process of socialization, or moral education, should take? Should these decisions be made, as Skinner has suggested, by an elite group of experts? Should they be made democratically by those who will be most directly affected? Or are decisions of this kind beyond the competence of any human group, and are we thus better off putting our trust in tradition and impersonal historical forces? If human groups are to make these decisions, what should the decision-making mechanism be?

Second, how can we determine what the nature of social influences on the individual should be? Presumably, some social influences favor individual freedom; some impede individual freedom; and some are compatible with individual freedom but neither favor nor impede it. Is there, however, a reliable method for discovering into which category any given form of social control or influence fits? To say, for example, that society should educate and guide individuals rather than to propagandize and regiment them does not take us very far. The fact that language permits us to make distinctions of this kind indicates that most of us do believe in desirable as well as undesirable social influences or controls. But specific measures that some applaud as education and guidance, others decry as propaganda and regimentation. For example, B. F. Skinner, who is probably better known than any other contemporary social thinker for his belief in the pervasiveness of social influences on the individual and the need consciously to shape and control the nature of those influences, has become the center of a storm of controversy every time he has tried to specify clearly which forms of social control are legitimate and which illegitimate.

The fact that these practical issues are still highly controversial ought not, however, to be taken as a reason for rejecting either (a) the position that social influence on the individual is inevitable and pervasive or (b) the position that social influence properly exercised can augment individual freedom. A philosophically sound position may well generate acutely difficult practical problems.

In dealing with these issues great care must also be taken not to fall into linguistic traps. As we have seen, terms like "social education" and "social guidance" have a favorable ring to them whereas terms like "propaganda" and "regimentation" have an unfavorable ring. Yet the specific meanings of these terms vary greatly from one person to another. The same is true of the specific meanings attaching to terms such as "freedom" and "oppression." In fact, although Skinner does favor freedom and dignity in some of the meanings of "freedom" and "dignity," he feels that these terms so strongly suggest views with which he disagrees—for example, those of Dostoevsky—that he gave one of his books the provocative title of *Beyond Freedom and Dignity.*

Material Prosperity

Since the Industrial Revolution greater material prosperity, or economic well-being, has been a widely acknowledged social goal. This is not surprising in view of the many obviously desirable goods and services made possible by modern technology and more efficient modes of production. First, there are those many things that promote good health, extend our life spans, and relieve physical pain: better food, shelter, clothing, drugs, surgical methods, nursing care, and so forth. Second, there are those many things that introduce greater pleasure into our lives: boats, sporting goods, theatres, recreation centers, movies, and so forth. Third, there are technological innovations and labor-saving devices that make it possible to eliminate many forms of drudgery and to increase our leisure. Fourth, there are goods and services that expand our intellectual and social horizons, making more of the world available to us: modern schools and teaching methods, printing presses, laboratories, improved transportation and communication systems, and so forth.

Moreover, it has been argued that progressively higher levels of material prosperity tend to ease social tension by reconciling people to real or fancied injustices in the distribution of wealth. Persons who each year find themselves better off materially than they were the year before are not likely to feel victimized by material inequalities. In a period of slow growth or recession, however, material inequalities often create acute social tensions, as the economically underprivileged aggressively demand a greater share of the national wealth.

Despite the impressive case in favor of ever higher levels of economic well-being a number of social critics, especially in the affluent capitalist countries, have expressed grave doubts about greater economic well-being as a valid social objective. One argument is that the very same technology and modes of production that have brought us undeniable material benefits have also brought us monstrous ills. Indeed, the list of evils to which modern technology and production methods have contributed is impressively long: the threat of atomic warfare, air pollution, traffic jams, oil spills, damage to the ecological balance, neighborhoods ruined by the flight patterns of ear-splitting aircraft, and so forth.

Advocates of continued economic growth counter this argument in either or both of two ways. First, they argue that the negative side effects of economic growth are an acceptable cost to pay for its many benefits. Second, they argue that many of these side effects are the consequence not of technology itself but of its misuse and that the appropriate remedy is to devise means of protecting ourselves against its misuse. Socialists in particular stress this second point. The misuse of technology, they say, is due primarily to the fact that in capitalist societies decisions regarding the use of technology are made by private individuals or corporations for the sake of private profit rather than by society itself in the public interest.

For example, consider air pollution and traffic jams. These ills are not only the result of technology. They are also the result of human decisions such as those favoring a system of transportation by private automobile over a public transportation system. More specifically, they are due to decisions by big corporations that make greater profits from the production of private automobiles. The proposed socialist solution, therefore, is to devise a political and economic system in which decisions of this kind are made by responsible public bodies.

A second argument against continued economic growth consists in the claim that economic growth fosters new needs and wants more rapidly than it satisfies old needs and wants. The result is a sense of frustration that more than cancels out any genuine benefits of economic growth. In other words, rapid economic growth does not close the gap between what we have and what we want but actually extends the gap. It leads not to fulfillment but merely to rising expectations.

This second argument is also countered in two different ways. One is to point out that the argument presupposes an unduly narrow and crude concept of human unhappiness as a matter of unfulfilled desire. Actually many of us have distant material goals toward which we are moving without the slightest sense of frustration or psychological discomfort. Unfulfilled wants are not necessarily a source of frustration. Frustration comes rather from an improper balance between chosen goals and the possibility of satisfying them. We noted this in Chapter One. We also noted that striking the proper balance between what we have and what we want is only one of many elements in human well-being. Increased pleasure and improved health, for example, are goods to which material prosperity definitely contributes. And it may well be that if the price for these goods is a measure of frustration, the price is worth paying. Certainly, the person whose life has been saved as a result of technological advances in medical treatment will be inclined to wonder whether frustration due to rising expectations is a sufficient reason for curbing technological advances.

The second answer presupposes substantial truth in the claim that economic growth has produced excessive expectations and frustrations. But, it is said, economic growth as such is not the culprit. The causes are certain features of advanced capitalist economies such as extensive advertising, installment buying, and an unduly competitive mentality that obliges everyone to keep up with the Joneses. And the solution, once again, is said to be a reform or overhaul of our political and economic institutions.

Chapter 3

Good Government

Just as a good society tends to maximize personal well-being, so a good government tends to promote a good society—that is, a society with a maximum of stability, harmony, cohesion, justice, freedom, and material well-being. But what are the proper limits of government? Do individuals have certain rights that governments should rarely, if ever, restrict? What role should the government play in the economic life of the nation? How and to what extent should citizens participate in making decisions of social significance? These are the kinds of questions that will be discussed in this chapter.

Individual and Human Rights

Most nations pay at least lip service to the idea of individual rights, or the notion that citizens should be able to engage in certain types of behavior without government restriction or penalty. Moreover, there is substantial agreement as to the kinds of behavior that ought to be immune from government restraints. Historically, the most important of these generally recognized individual rights—also called natural rights, civil liberties, and civil rights—are freedom of speech, freedom of movement, freedom to choose one's occupation, freedom of religion, freedom of association or assembly, and freedom from arbitrary arrest or imprisonment.

Despite widespread agreement on general principles, there are considerable differences in interpretation and practice. For example, although almost everybody agrees that there should be freedom of religion, there is controversy as to whether exemptions from military service should be granted because of religious beliefs and as to whether religious organizations should be exempt from taxes. Similarly, although almost everyone agrees to the principle of freedom of speech, an attack on a government official that some persons would defend in the name of free speech others would condemn as a case of slander. Again, although almost everyone agrees to the principle of freedom of association, there is sharp disagreement as to whether this right should be extended to political organizations subsidized by a foreign power or advocating the violent overthrow of the existing government.

In the Anglo-American philosophical tradition there have been two major justifications of individual rights. The earlier and historically more influential of these is the theory of *inalienable natural rights,* or rights that belong to all of us and that we may not legitimately transfer to others. The foremost advocate of this theory was the seventeenth-century English philosopher John Locke, whose influence is evident in the Constitution of the United States. Locke took over from Thomas Hobbes the distinction between a state of nature and our actual social state. He also took over from Hobbes the view that the relationship between the individual and the government is in the nature of a contract, called the *social contract.* As Hobbes saw it, the conditions of life in a state of nature are so horrible that rational individuals could see the need for a strong government authority and would gladly surrender their natural rights to the government in return for personal security and social harmony. Unlike Hobbes, however, Locke strongly insisted that rational individuals would value their freedom too much to surrender more than a few of their natural rights. According to Locke, therefore, a valid social contract that provides for the transfer of some natural rights to the government must also provide that many natural rights be retained by the individual parties to the contract. These retained natural rights are the inalienable natural rights.

It appears that many of the persons who originally advanced the theory of inalienable natural rights believed that there was actually a time when human beings lived in a state of nature and that the social contract was a real historical event. But even in the seventeenth century these beliefs had only wavering support, and today we know beyond any reasonable doubt that they are false. Human beings have always lived in communities and have always been subject to social restraints. There is even good reason for believing that social restraints on the individual were stronger in the distant past than they are today. Theories of inalienable natural rights, therefore, are usually interpreted as answers to the following hypothetical questions: If one *were* in a state of nature and if one *were* fully rational, what rights would one find it in one's interest to renounce in favor of the government, providing that all other individuals did the same? And what rights would one find it in one's interest to retain for oneself and to accord to all other individuals?

This approach to the problem of individual rights is defended on two grounds. First, many social contract theorists believe that legitimate individual rights belong to us simply because of our humanity —or by virtue of human "nature" in the Aristotelian sense discussed in Chapter One—and not as a result of particular historical or social circumstances. Therefore, it is only in an ahistorical and asocial state of nature that these individual rights could be determined. If we attempted to determine what individual rights are legitimate by examining the actual historical circumstances in the United States, the Soviet Union, or some other contemporary society, there would be no guarantee that the catalogue we came up with would have absolute and universal validity.

Second, if we examine the views about individual rights that people actually hold, we find that these views have in most cases been profoundly influenced by social prejudice and self-interest. Millionaires, for example, tend to find it self-evident that the right to earn a million dollars is inalienable. The poor are less convinced. It is only, therefore, by stripping away particular historical and social circumstances until we discover the irreducible core of the human condition that we can make unbiased and disinterested judgments about individual rights. In the words of the American philosopher John Rawls, the foremost contemporary advocate of social contract theory, a decision about the rights to which individuals have legitimate claims can be made only after we have placed before our eyes "a veil of ignorance."

Critics of the doctrine of inalienable natural rights tend to make two major points. First, they reject the notion of a common or universal human nature. The human species, like other animal species, has no fixed nature. It is constantly evolving. Moreover, this evolutionary process, as it works itself out in the human species, is essentially historical. There are, therefore, no absolute or universal individual rights. The legitimate rights of individuals are always relative to the particular historical and social circumstances of their society.

Second, since there never was a state of nature, an attempt to determine what individual rights rational individuals in a state of nature would insist on retaining is considered unduly speculative. Some critics go even further and say that the attempt is absurd. The only satisfactory basis for a judgment regarding individual rights is that very particular social-historical context in which we actually find ourselves and which the natural rights theorists tell us we ought to ignore. Surely, a society at war or in the throes of revolutionary upheaval is not going to adopt a veil of ignorance in order to determine whether individual rights should be abridged or suspended. And it is difficult to see why a judgment to suspend or abridge, let us say, freedom of speech in wartime would necessarily be biased or self-interested. It could, indeed, be plausibly maintained that unbiased and disinterested judgments require the fullest possible knowledge of the particular historical-social context.

The second major justification of individual rights in the Anglo-American tradition is utilitarianism. According to the utilitarian view individuals should be granted those rights and only those rights whose exercise would lead to the greatest happiness of the greatest number. Decisions as to what rights individuals should enjoy as well as decisions relating to when and in what respects those rights should be suspended or abridged can only be made after a careful effort to evaluate the results of these decisions in terms of social utility. One of the consequences of the utilitarian view is that detailed justifications of specific individual rights follow different patterns, since different kinds of individual rights tend to be useful in different ways. The social utility of freedom of movement, for example, is not of the same sort as the social utility of freedom of speech. A related consequence is that detailed justifications of each kind of individual right are fairly complex and normally involve a weighing, or balancing, of advantages and disadvantages. For the social effects of almost any specific individual right are numerous and include both favorable and unfavorable features.

John Stuart Mill's famous defense of freedom of speech is an example of a utilitarian justification of one kind of individual right. Mill starts from the generally accepted premise that any society—but particularly a democratic society—will benefit enormously from a widespread knowledge of the truth regarding major social policies. The substance of his argument is that the truth is more likely to emerge and more likely to be widely accepted in a society that grants all individuals the right to express their views, no matter how unpopular, than in a society that denies this right.

Mill offers three principal reasons in support of this contention. First, no matter how widely accepted and firmly held an opinion may be, it is always possible that the opinion is false. To deny dissenters the right to speak out against the accepted view may, therefore, lead society to perpetuate a social prejudice and to reduce chances of discovering the truth. Second, questions of social policy are usually complex, as are the positions held with respect to these questions. Thus, even if the majority position is substantially correct, it does not follow that a knowledge of minority positions would be useless. The minority position could still contain elements of truth. For example, even if it were the case that capitalism is superior to socialism, or vice versa, it would not follow that capitalists and socialists had nothing to learn from one another. Marx did not hesitate to acknowledge a debt to capitalist economists, and it would be surprising if contemporary capitalist economists had nothing to learn from their socialist colleagues. Finally, even if the majority position were the truth and the whole truth in regard to a given question, there would still be a social gain in obliging those who hold it to defend that position against intelligent and informed critics. As Socrates pointed out in the fourth century B.C., there is a vast difference between "true opinion" and "genuine knowledge," between just happening to hold the right view and holding the right view for the right reasons. Persons who just happen to be capitalists or socialists because capitalism or socialism is the dominant view in their society would be putty in the hands of an enemy bent on brainwashing them. As Socrates said, right opinion unlike true knowledge cannot be "tied down." It "runs away" from us. Only individuals who have examined their position in depth under the prodding of serious critics can claim really to know it, and only they can lay a reasonable claim to a genuine and vital belief in that position.

Mill recognized that freedom of speech could lead to the triumph of a false minority position. It could be that advocates of a false minority view are more persuasive than the advocates of a true majority view. But this danger, he reasoned, is far less than the danger of mindlessly perpetuating false popular prejudices by silencing critics of conventional views. Mill also recognized that freedom of speech was not absolute and had to be limited. The social disadvantages of slander and of allowing persons to shout "Fire!" in a crowded hall are obvious. But the real danger, as he saw it, lies not in the absence of universal and absolute individual rights but rather in the lack of a rational basis for determining the proper limits of individual rights.

Criticism of the utilitarian position on individual rights will be presented in Chapter Six when we discuss the general doctrine of utilitarianism. At this point we shall turn to some criticisms of what is sometimes called the *social contract model of society.* According to this view of society, the principal actors on the social scene are (a) independent, rational individual agents, each with very limited power, and (b) a powerful government whose powers derive from a surrender of natural rights by individuals. The social contract model was clearly part of the background of the original doctrine of inalienable individual rights. And, although it is not essential to utilitarianism, many contemporary utilitarians—especially those of socialist leanings—claim that Mill and the other classical utilitarians were unduly influenced by it.

The social contract model is said to be misleading in two ways: First, it does not allow for the fact that in most societies the government is but one of several institutional centers of power and not necessarily the strongest. In many ancient civilizations—Egypt, for example—a priest class was dominant and the government was hardly more than its tool. During the Middle Ages and the early modern period in most European countries national governments exercised much less power than the feudal aristocracies. And in capitalist societies of today big business is often alleged to be more powerful than government.

This failure to take nongovernmental centers of power into account is said to be dangerous insofar as it leads us to assume that individual rights are exclusively or primarily matters of freedom from governmental, or legal, restraints. In fact, nongovernmental restrictions on individual rights can be just as oppressive as governmental restrictions. This point was anticipated in the preceding chapter when it was said that the freedom of the individual is limited by all sorts of negative sanctions, not only legal sanctions but material and moral sanctions as well. To equate the freedom of the individual with the mere absence of government sanctions is thus to ignore the true plight of the individual in search of freedom.

Moreover, by ignoring nongovernmental centers of power we are led to overlook the positive role the government can play in securing individual rights against other agents of oppression. For example, the excesses of the French Revolutionary government and its abuses of individual rights are well known. We easily forget, however, that it was this same revolutionary government that permanently broke the back of the oppressive feudal system with its systematic denial of individual rights. We see the revolutionary government's role as tyrant, but so long as we ignore the power of the feudal aristocracy we do not see the government's role as liberator.

Take a contemporary example. Consider the situation of someone in the United States today who holds a minority political position that threatens big business. We can reasonably assume that this person wishes to bring that position to the attention of those who favor big business. And, if we agree with John Stuart Mill, the expression of this minority view has little social utility unless it reaches the intended audience. What, then, will be the value of the mere absence of legal restrictions on this person's freedom of speech? If the situation today were similar to what it was in the early and middle part of the nineteenth century when Mill was writing, the absence of legal restraints would probably be crucial. At that time, the power to influence public opinion was widely diffused. No group could easily monopolize the media, and many people could, if sufficiently determined, reach a significant segment of the public. The principal media were the thousands of newspapers published throughout the nation. If a person of modest means could not get a minority view published in an existing newspaper, the cost of starting a new one was not prohibitive. Today, however, the situation is radically different. Newspapers have dwindled in number, and the cost of launching a new one is prohibitive to all but the very wealthy. Furthermore, today's newspapers are themselves big businesses and they depend on other big businesses as advertisers for their survival. The same is true for the TV networks, which have eclipsed the newspapers as opinion makers. Can we, therefore, reasonably expect that the critic of big business will be given a significant voice in today's media? What social value does the individual's legal right to express antibusiness views have if the media deny access? And how can private individuals opposed to big business hope to secure access to unwilling media if not through political pressure or government action?

The second way in which the social contract model allegedly misleads is by its assumption that individuals are wholly independent agents with a capacity for rational decision that owes nothing to social and historical circumstances. Since there is no process of socialization and no socially structured environment in a state of nature, the patterns of individuals' wants and desires would be determined entirely by their private individual histories. And since according to the social contract model the government is the only significant social power and exercises only those powers expressly granted to it, even in the social state individuals are substantially independent of social forces.

Thus, under the influence of the social contract model, John Stuart Mill made a sharp distinction between the private life and the public life of an individual—or between individual acts without social ramifications and individual acts with social ramifications. Mill actually seemed to believe that private actions outnumber public actions. Furthermore, in discussing individual rights Mill often substituted for the utilitarian justification a justification in terms of this distinction between private and public actions. Everyone, he claimed, has not only a right but an "absolute right" to do as one pleases in one's private life or in what concerns only oneself. Critics of the Anglo-American tradition seem, therefore, to be right in attributing to the entire tradition—including classical utilitarianism—not only a neglect of nongovernmental centers of power but also an unduly heavy stress upon the independence of the individual vis-à-vis society. Moreover, the two emphases tend to go together. For the substantial independence of the individual becomes a plausible doctrine only if we overlook nongovernmental centers of power and confuse the larger concept of society with the narrower concept of government.

But why is it dangerous to overstress the independence of the individual? Critics of the Anglo-American tradition answer that it is dangerous because it leads to the mistaken belief that society can best promote individual freedom by allowing individuals to do whatever they happen to desire, or by satisfying whatever wants they happen to have. In economics this belief is often referred to as the principle of *consumer sovereignty*. Thus, for example, most English-speaking people tend to think that a high level of violence in TV programming can be justified if most people want that kind of programming. In a free society, it is said, the public ought to get the TV programs it wants. But what if the desire for violence in TV programs has itself been nurtured by the TV networks, who in order to reach the widest possible audience and to obtain the greatest possible income from advertising deliberately appealed to the worst rather than the best in human nature? What if the effect of a high level of violence on TV is to increase the level of violence in real life and thereby frustrate the basic need for a more harmonious social order? And what if individuals are unaware both of the extent to which their craving for violent TV programs has been socially conditioned and of the injury to their own best long-range interests that these programs represent?

Consider another example. Most individuals in the United States today prefer private automobiles to public transportation. It is, therefore, often taken for granted on the basis of the principle of consumer sovereignty that the good society must satisfy this demand. But why should this be taken for granted? Many people claim that the widespread desire to own a car is due to the fact that the automobile industry has bombarded the public with misleading advertising campaigns and has used its substantial power and influence to discourage the development of quick, comfortable, clean, and inexpensive forms of public transportation. The widespread use of private automobiles is said to be socially pernicious. Public transportation has a much better safety record, uses considerably less energy, and pollutes less. At the same time it has been argued that the widespread desire for private automobiles is sick or irrational: the automobile represents not a needed mode of transportation but a status symbol in a highly competitive and self-defeating game of oneupmanship. It may, therefore, be that rather than satisfy the desire for private automobiles, society ought to (a) counter the automobile industry's advertising campaign with a government-sponsored public education program, (b) make public transportation more attractive by appropriating more tax money toward this end, and (c) discourage the use of private automobiles by increasing retail sales taxes on gasoline.

The claims and recommendations of those who oppose violence on television and heavy dependence on private automobiles may be false or misguided. Whether they are is irrelevant to this discussion. The point is that since individual desires are publicly shaped either by some process of social education in the broad sense of that term, which includes advertising, or else by some form of environmental structuring, it is essential that attention be paid to the social influences on the formation of individual desires. Responsible efforts must be made to identify these influences and to understand their consequences. And it must be recognized that just as government may play a positive role in liberating human beings from nongovernmental sources of oppression, so it may play a positive role in the formation of fully rational, individually wholesome, and socially acceptable desires.

Thus, as we noted earlier, many contemporary utilitarians—especially those who are also socialists—attack not only the theory of inalienable individual rights but also what they judge to be an antigovernment bias in the elaboration of the utilitarian position by John Stuart Mill and other classical utilitarians. These critics do not ordinarily deny that governments can and often do abuse their powers, arbitrarily obstructing the pursuit of happiness and unnecessarily reducing the number of social options. But, they insist, the abuse of government power is neither the only nor necessarily the most dangerous threat to individual freedom. And, often, social circumstances are such that government alone is in a position to promote true individual freedom, be it freedom from restraint or freedom of choice.

Accordingly, in socialist countries discussions of individual rights give less emphasis to the evils of big government, stressing instead the need for an active government role in helping individuals to fulfill basic needs for such things as jobs, education, medical care, and clean air. The focus is not on what government should leave undone but on what government should do. The list of individual rights includes not only freedom of speech, freedom of religion, freedom of association, and so forth, but also the right to a job, to an education commensurate with one's talents regardless of family income, to adequate medical care, and so on. The individual's need for freedom from unwarranted legal restrictions is usually viewed as a matter of less urgency than the individual's need for a responsible government that takes a position of leadership in the moral education, or socialization, of the individual and that actively works to structure a social environment capable of bringing out the best in human nature.

Because the term "individual rights" has so often been used by advocates of limited, or minimal, government and because its history so insistently suggests what many see as a one-sided concern for legal as opposed to material and moral freedom, many people since World War II use the expression "human rights" instead. This is especially true in international forums such as the United Nations and UNESCO. Those who prefer the term "human rights" usually distinguish between two groups of rights. The first, called "civil and political rights," correspond closely to the more traditional individual rights such as freedom of religion, freedom of assembly, and freedom from arbitrary arrest. For the most part these are rights to be left alone, or to be protected from improper government action. The second group of human rights, called "social and economic rights," includes such things as the right to medical care, to a job, and to an education appropriate to one's talents. In general, these are rights to assistance, or help, and imply a positive obligation on the part of government. Unfortunately, this useful distinction is being blurred today in the Western capitalist nations, where a number of influential public figures have appropriated the term "human rights" and use it as a rough synonym for "individual rights."

Before closing this section we should note that not all opponents of big government underestimate the strength of nongovernmental centers of power or overestimate the extent of individual independence from social controls. Many advocates of limited, or minimal, government are as convinced as any socialist that historical and social circumstances shape the individual's life. They do not, therefore, automatically assume that the alternative to government power is individual freedom. Rather, they argue that the government is a more dangerous or less effective instrument of social control than alternative instruments such as family, church, private business, tradition, or impersonal historical forces. For example, with regard to the government's proper role in the economic life of the nation not all opponents of big government simply assume that the alternative to government controls over the economy is economic freedom for the individual. Some grant that the economic life of an individual is always and necessarily circumscribed by forces largely beyond that individual's control. And they agree that the true alternatives to government planning are impersonal market forces or nongovernment centers of economic power such as business corporations. Furthermore, they see clearly that the person who loses a job because of a business recession can thereby suffer as great a material disadvantage as the person who has been fired by a government bureaucrat. Accordingly, they build their case for limited government not on a simplistic dichotomy between the public and the private, or between the government and the individual, but rather on a comparative assessment of the pros and cons of government controls as against the pros and cons of practical alternatives to government controls.

Depending on the areas of life affected and historical circumstances, the alternatives to governmental controls take many different forms. Therefore, the arguments for or against government controls are also varied. There are, however, several general considerations that those who favor limited government—or the minimal state—frequently bring up. First, the reach of the government is greater than the reach of most alternative agents of power. Laws apply to everyone within a nation's boundaries. Only by a drastic step such as voluntary exile may individuals remove themselves from their influence. An organization such as a church or a private business corporation exercises power within a smaller sphere from which individuals may ordinarily remove themselves at considerably less cost or sacrifice. Second, every law is ultimately backed by the police and military establishments—that is, by the coercive power of the state in the form of brute physical force. Only a very few nongovernmental centers of power—for example, organized crime operating outside of the law—use brute physical force. Finally, when a society chooses to rely on impersonal forces such as a free market economy rather than government planning, any personal misfortunes that result from this decision are likely to do less damage to the social fabric. The victims of faulty government planning tend to perceive their misfortunes as social injustices and harbor resentment against the social agents of their misfortunes. The victims of impersonal market forces, on the contrary, often react to their misfortunes as they would to an act of God or to a natural catastrophe.

The rejoinders of those who tend to favor government controls over other instruments or agents of social control presuppose that governments can and should be genuinely democratic. First, whereas government controls in a democracy are instituted by those affected to further their own interests, nongovernmental controls—for example, impersonal market forces or private business corporations—are usually beyond the reach and direction of those whose lives they affect. Second, although all governments can and on occasion do secure obedience to the law by the threat or exercise of brute physical force, genuine democratic governments rule primarily by force of moral authority. Ordinary citizens in a democratic society do not obey the laws because they are afraid of being jailed but rather because they believe that the laws are just and that government officials have a legitimate right to impose them. Finally, it is said that in a truly democratic society social injustices due to faulty government decisions do not pose serious threats to the social order. For the victims of injustice know that inept or unjust governments may be replaced and that wrongs to individuals or groups may be righted through orderly political processes.

Laissez-faire Capitalism

There are many positions on the proper role of government in the economic affairs of the nation, and unfortunately there is no standard or fully satisfactory vocabulary for designating them. For our purposes in this book we shall divide these positions into two major groups. Theories according to which most means of production should be owned by private individuals or corporations and managed for the profit of the owners will be called *capitalist*. Theories according to which the principal means of production should be publicly owned and managed will be called *socialist*.

One of the first champions of capitalism—and historically the most influential—was the Scottish philosopher and economist Adam Smith, who advocated a form of capitalism known as *laissez-faire capitalism*. According to his major work, *The Wealth of Nations*, first published in 1776, the government has three and only three proper roles: the defense of the nation against foreign enemies, the protection of individual persons and their property against fraud and physical violence, and the exercise of a small number of economic activities that private individuals can not profitably undertake. The principal corollary of this view is that individuals or voluntary groups of individuals should be legally free to manufacture almost any product and to render almost any service from which they can hope to make a profit. It is for this reason that Smith's view is called *laissez-faire* capitalism, "laissez faire" being a French expression meaning to let (people) do (as they please). Like most other advocates of laissez-faire capitalism, Smith was vague about the kinds of enterprises that do not promise sufficient reward to private owners and must therefore be financed out of the public treasury. He mentioned only harbors and education. By definition, however, all advocates of laissez faire regard such enterprises as limited in number.

It has often been pointed out that no society has conformed fully to the plan of the laissez-faire theorists. In Smith's day most European governments subscribed to a policy known as *mercantilism*, which provided for fairly systematic government regulation of business in order to promote a favorable international balance of trade. Moreover, as mercantilist regulation decreased during the Industrial Revolution, governments often imposed different forms of regulation in an effort to solve new problems. Nonetheless, England and the United

States in the nineteenth century are usually regarded as fairly close approximations to the laissez-faire ideal.

Smith's principal defense of laissez-faire capitalism was that a hands-off policy on the part of government would result in the highest possible level of material well-being. He argued roughly as follows: As long as many different businesses compete for the same market and as long as anyone with a relatively small sum of capital is free to enter into this competition, established businesses must make a serious effort to sell the best quality products at the lowest possible prices. For if a business produces inferior goods or overprices its goods, existing or new competitors will take over its share of the market and force it to close its doors. And, of course, constant efforts by many businesses to produce the best product at the lowest possible price encourages efficiency in modes of production and technological advances from which society as a whole profits. At the same time, the competitive struggle prevents owners of businesses from collecting excessive profits.

As Smith emphasized, his formula for producing the greatest possible sum of material well-being for all was remarkable in that it seemed to call for no real sacrifices from anybody. Consumers and owners of businesses alike were to be motivated by nothing but economic self-interest. Consumers obviously want the highest quality goods for the lowest possible prices; but so do the owners of businesses, since only by marketing quality goods at low prices can they make a profit. It is as if an "invisible hand" controls the competitive market system, ensuring that the socially desirable good of material prosperity is achieved by nothing other than the independent, calculated pursuit of individual self-interest.

The most important criticisms of laissez-faire capitalism are as follows:

The Degradation of Labor. Smith wrote as if the most important segments of the economic community were sellers and buyers. Propertyless workers, who in Smith's day were already well on the way to becoming the most important single group in capitalist societies, were virtually ignored except as sellers of labor power and buyers of goods and services. Yet their plight, especially at the zenith of laissez-faire capitalism, was pitiful. As a rule, wages were barely enough to permit workers to maintain their health and to raise families. Periods of unemployment were frequent and unpredictable. Thousands of teen-age and even pre-teen-age children worked as much as fourteen hours a day in unhealthy mines, often dying before reaching maturity.

Moreover, even if workers under capitalism received adequate material rewards and security, their work would still be demeaning. For unlike artisans or craft workers of precapitalist days, factory workers under capitalism have no control over the work process. In the language of Marx the workers are "alienated from the product of their labor" insofar as they have no voice in its design, its mode of production, or its final disposition. Workers under capitalism are merely cogs in a large-scale productive process that is owned and managed by a few individuals for private profit.

This last point must not be misunderstood. Most socialists believe that large-scale productive processes under capitalism often involve unnecessarily specialized and excessively mechanized or routine tasks because the owners want to maintain tight control over the workers. It is not in the interests of the owners that workers learn enough about the productive process to enable them to take over the managerial functions. Each worker's role must, therefore, be made as specialized and routine as possible. It is only under socialism, when the workers themselves become owners, that this capitalist tendency toward overspecialization and overroutinization can be overcome. Most socialists also believe, however, that the efficient use of modern technology demands many large-scale productive processes, which in turn require greater specialization and, possibly, routinization of the work process than in precapitalist days. For Marx, techniques of mass production and technological improvements are capitalism's most positive contributions to historical progress.

Accordingly, when socialists talk about the dehumanization, degradation, or alienation of the worker, the basic emphasis is usually on the fact that workers have no voice regarding the work process in which they are engaged. In precapitalist days productive laborers— for example, carpenters—owned their own tools and managed their own affairs. Under capitalism, however, ownership and management have been divorced from the productive work process. On the one hand, there are many productive laborers who own nothing and who work in large-scale enterprises such as modern factories at tasks set for them by others. On the other hand, there are a small number of individuals who own the principal means of production and manage them entirely for private profit. For Marx the emergence of owner-managers as a separate class is one of the basic "contradictions" of capitalism. It is also, perhaps, the feature of capitalism that best explains how it differs not only from the precapitalist economy out of which it evolved but also from the socialist economy that Marx expected to replace it. The basic differences among the three types of economy are represented schematically in the following chart, where the word "public" means not governmental but rather social or collective.

	Mode of Production	Ownership and Management
Precapitalist	Private	Private
Capitalist	Public	Private
Socialist	Public	Public

Business Cycles. Smith believed that in a laissez-faire economy the level of production would expand rapidly and steadily. He was half-right. The rate of industrial growth in England and America was much greater in the nineteenth century under laissez faire than ever before and much greater than the rate of growth in the twentieth century under the modified forms of capitalism that replaced laissez faire. However, expansion during this remarkable period of growth was anything but steady. Instead, there were periods of feverish economic activity followed by crises and depressions of considerable magnitude. These business cycles have continued up to the present time and are still poorly understood. But there is no question that the unusually high levels of unemployment, the stock market declines, the bank failures, and the business bankruptcies that normally characterize the low phases of the business cycles produce numerous personal tragedies. And so do the inflationary periods that characterize the peaks of these cycles, especially for those on pensions or other fixed incomes and those who are heavily dependent on past savings. It is also clear that the general unpredictability of the business cycles produces constant insecurity and anxiety not only for workers but for the owners and managers as well.

Monopoly and Oligopoly. Smith contended that under laissez-faire capitalism the number of sellers and buyers of any given commodity would be sufficiently numerous and the size of the units involved sufficiently small that (a) no one buyer or seller could control the price of that commodity and (b) anyone with a small sum of capital would be in a position to join the competition. In other words, the price of a commodity would be determined by impersonal market forces, or the laws of supply and demand. And, of course, as we have seen, competition in this impersonal market dominated by the laws of supply and demand was supposed to guarantee low prices. But already in the nineteenth century the market failed to live up to this ideal of "perfect competition." In a number of industries monopolies emerged. In others, oligopolies, or a few giant corporations with a tendency to adopt similar pricing policies, assumed control. At the same time governments emerged as big buyers, particularly in the military supply and transportation industries. And cooperative government procurement officials often helped the monopolies and oligopolies consolidate their power. The result was price-fixing rather than price competition and much higher prices than would have obtained under conditions of perfect competition.

Unethical Sales Practices. Smith believed that competition among businesses would revolve not only around prices but also around the quality of the product. This belief followed from the assumption that typical buyers would be able to identify the qualitatively superior products from among the competing products offered for sale. This assumption was reasonably safe in Smith's day. But, as the technological sophistication of products offered to the public has increased, this assumption has come into serious question. Few people know how to evaluate the relative merits of different cars, TV sets, kitchen appliances, and nonprescription drugs. And there is evidence that even doctors often cannot evaluate the relative merits of competing prescription drugs.

Thus, competition among businesses becomes increasingly a matter of style rather than substance, of advertising pitch or packaging rather than of quality. And the public is increasingly victimized by dishonest practices. In auto repair, for example, few customers can verify that they have received the services for which they have paid. Moreover, there is considerable evidence that manufacturers deliberately produce shoddy products, expecting to be able to make additional profits on early replacements. This "built-in obsolescence," as it is called, is reputed to be especially common in industries controlled by oligopolies. Closely related to this last practice is a tendency of capitalists with a vested interest in a given product to suppress technological innovations to protect an existing source of profit.

Excessive Profits. Because, according to Smith, owners of businesses had to make a product of sufficiently high quality and offer it at a sufficiently low price to be competitive, the level of their profits would be reasonably low and could be justified as a reward for a socially useful service. To the extent, however, that price fixing replaces price competition and that competitive advantages cease to be related to the quality of the product, business profits tend to become greater and there ceases to be any satisfactory basis for justifying the gap between the income of the business owner or industrialist and the worker or welfare recipient. There is no reason for society to reward those who manipulate the market, produce inferior goods, and mislead the public with deceptive advertising and other unethical practices.

The Misuse of Technology. Technological and industrial advance has brought with it a number of unintended and deplorable side effects. Among them are pollution of the environment with industrial wastes, earsplitting jackhammers and jet airplanes, ugly billboard advertising, traffic jams, and electrical blackouts. To some extent these side effects may represent an unavoidable cost for the benefits of technology. But, as we saw in the last chapter, critics of capitalism argue that most of them are due not so much to technology as to business competition and the unrestricted pursuit of private profit. For example, the technology that has produced noisy jackhammers has also produced relatively silent jackhammers. But since the latter are more expensive and since the public that suffers from the use of the noisy variety has no effective voice under laissez-faire capitalism, the business owners who decide which variety to use invariably prefer the one providing them with a competitive cost advantage. The social cost is borne by the public.

Welfare Capitalism

In view of the many unhappy developments under the largely laissez-faire nineteenth-century economy it was inevitable that there should be attempts to modify the workings of capitalism. The result of these efforts is often called *welfare capitalism.* The corrective measures adopted under welfare capitalism are of many different kinds, and originally at least they were all strongly opposed by the business community and the big corporations. Societies that have gone a long way on the path of welfare capitalism are sometimes called socialist even though most businesses and industries remain in private hands and continue to be operated for private profit. Sweden, for example, despite a substantial private sector, is often labeled socialist because it deviates so much from the laissez-faire ideal. Although we do not challenge the appropriateness of this use of the word "socialist," it should be noted that it does not accord with the use adopted in this book. As we are using the term, socialism requires predominantly public ownership and management.

One of the first challenges to laissez-faire capitalism was the trade-union movement. Today unionism is taken more or less for granted in almost all capitalist countries, and there is general agreement that unionism is responsible for much-needed improvements in the wages and working conditions of labor. In its early days, however, unionism was bitterly opposed. The basic argument against unionism is that labor power is itself a commodity and that if the capitalist system is to succeed in its principal goal of increasing the supply of moderately priced quality goods labor power must be treated in the same way as any other commodity. If working people, the suppliers of labor power, were allowed through union activity to monopolize their commodity and protect it against competition, the cost of labor power would increase inordinately and force up the cost of all other commodities.

Champions of labor argue in rebuttal that higher wages are passed along to the consumer in the form of higher prices only to the extent that competition has broken down and been replaced by monopolistic or oligopolistic control of the market. Where competition is genuine higher wages are paid for out of excess business profits. Champions of labor also argue that the major effect of higher wages is to stimulate business activity, since higher wages are returned to the market in the form of greater purchasing power by labor. If workers were not well paid, the suppliers of commodities would have too few buyers with too little money and market activity would be disastrously suppressed. Whatever the merits of these respective arguments, almost all capitalist governments today have reversed their original opposition to labor unions, giving them legal status and protection.

About the same time that capitalist governments began to accept labor unions, they also enacted a great deal of welfare legislation, from which the term "welfare capitalism" is derived. Welfare legislation includes not only what we today call "welfare" but also minimum wage laws to protect unorganized labor, workmen's compensation laws for the benefit of injured workers, unemployment compensation to tide over temporarily unemployed workers, some form of public medical care, government pensions for the aged, government insured savings accounts, free elementary and secondary schooling, financial aid for students in higher education, and so forth. Like actions taken on behalf of unions, these measures are seen primarily as necessary to correct some of the more inhumane consequences of laissez-faire capitalism.

Another function of contemporary capitalist governments is the protection of the consumer against false advertising, the sale of shoddy or unsafe goods, overpricing as a result of monopolistic or oligopolistic control of the market, and other questionable business practices. This activity is primarily the responsibility of government regulatory agencies.

Probably the most important of the efforts to correct the problems of the predominantly laissez-faire economies of capitalist countries in earlier days, however, are government attempts to control the evils of the business cycles. These attempts have ordinarily involved the use of what are called *indirect controls* over business activity. The chief indirect controls are fiscal—or taxation—policies and monetary—or money and credit—policies. The theoretical justification for the use of indirect controls was provided by the English economist John Maynard Keynes, who died in 1946. According to Keynes the inflation that tends to accompany periods of business prosperity may be reduced (a) by increasing taxes, thereby reducing available purchasing power and the demand for goods, and (b) by reducing the supply of money and credit, thereby denying businesses the funds needed to expand. In times of recession or depression, on the other hand, the government may stimulate production (a) by reducing taxes, thereby increasing purchasing power and the demand for goods, and (b) by increasing the supply of money and credit, thereby encouraging businesses to expand their activities.

Although some segments of the business community are still opposed to indirect, or Keynesian, controls, today most owners of businesses and almost all professional economists favor their use. Indeed, most economists credit the relatively long period of more or less sustained economic expansion in the capitalist world from the end of World War II into the 1970s to a judicious use of fiscal and monetary controls.

Moreover, many people currently favor what are called *direct controls*—that is, (a) government determination of wages and prices and (b) public works programs designed to give jobs to those who cannot find jobs in the private sector. In addition, more and more economists are coming to favor public planning commissions to gather statistics, to anticipate economic trends, and to recommend new ways to maintain healthy national economies.

Proponents of these various measures of welfare capitalism have been attacked both from the right and from the left. On the right are those who argue that laissez-faire capitalism never had a fair chance and that the alleged evils of laissez-faire capitalism are in fact the result of misguided efforts to correct them. If, it is argued, labor and government had exercised more restraint and allowed impersonal economic forces free rein, the so-called evils of capitalism would never have developed at all or would have disappeared in short order. Moreover, even if government intervention in the economic life of the nation could increase the general level of material prosperity, the price would be a totally unwarranted sacrifice of individual freedom.

From the left welfare capitalism has been attacked by the socialists, who claim that its remedies to the problems of laissez-faire capitalism are completely inadequate. Despite the labor movement and welfare measures, assert the socialists, the lot of workers in capitalist societies is still unenviable. If employed, their work is usually demeaning and their future insecure. If unemployed, they live in poverty and lose their self-respect. Despite government regulatory agencies business and industry still cheat the public, using their ill-gotten wealth to corrupt the regulators. And as to government controls, the simple fact is that after two hundred years of capitalism the business cycle is still very much with us and still as poorly understood as ever. In fact, many people say that business cycles are an even greater problem today than in the past. For contrary to all past experience recent recessions have not brought low prices but rather continued inflation. And *stagflation*—the combination of unusually high unemployment, underutilized industrial capacity, and inflation—is even less well understood than classical recession and cannot be adequately dealt with by either indirect or direct controls.

Socialism

Socialism, it will be remembered, calls for a society in which the principal means of production are owned and managed socially. This definition is vague in that it does not specify how large the social, or public, sector should be—or, putting it the other way around, how large a private sector should be permitted. In the Soviet Union, most East European countries, China, and Cuba the private sector consists almost entirely of single-family enterprises. But many socialists in the advanced capitalist nations have expressed a willingness to accept a much larger private sector.

This definition of "socialism" is also vague insofar as it does not specify exactly what "social," or "public," ownership and control means. Almost all socialists agree at least in principle that there should be a substantial measure of autonomy for individual plants and other relatively small economic units, with considerable decision-making power in the hands of democratically elected workers' councils. At the same time almost all socialists agree that the full benefits of socialism can be realized only if there is some degree of planning and supervision at the national level. But the proper mix of central planning and democratic decision making at the lower level and the proper means of making the national government genuinely responsible to the people are two highly controversial issues among socialists both within and without the socialist countries.

Socialists who strongly favor direct worker control at the place of work and a maximum of popular control over the national government often take a dim view of existing socialist societies, particularly the Soviet Union. In fact, many socialists refuse to call the Soviet Union a socialist society at all. Some even describe the Soviet system as "state capitalism," arguing that it is not significantly different from conventional capitalist societies. All that has happened, they say, is that state functionaries have replaced the old private owners and managers as the privileged class. These critics deny the official Soviet claim to have established worker control over the means of production. "Democratic" elections of local workers' councils, they say, are rigged; and in any case these councils have practically no power. The real power is in the hands of the national Communist Party and an entrenched national bureaucracy over which the people do not have even indirect control. The "democratic" national elections, claim these critics, are as much of a farce as the local elections in the work place.

It should also be noted that our definition of socialism does not imply any particular position with respect to the distribution of wealth. This is important because it is widely but erroneously believed that socialists by definition favor strict equality in the distribution of wealth. Actually, socialists who favor strict equality constitute a small minority. Most socialists believe, as did Marx, Engels, and Lenin, that for some time after the establishment of a socialist society material work incentives are required. It is only after a process of socialist reeducation and after scarcity has given way to abundance that material incentives and the inequalities that necessarily accompany them can be eliminated. And when socialist reeducation has been completed and material scarcities have been overcome, the primary criterion of distributive justice will be not equality but need. The formula most often used to characterize the socialist theory of justice for the later stage of socialist development is: "From each according to his ability, to each according to his need." And it should be noted that many socialists reserve the term "communism" to describe this later stage of socialist development, which no socialist country as yet claims to have achieved.

Nevertheless, most socialists do support even in the earlier stages of socialism a substantial narrowing of the gap between the rich and the poor as well as a greater reliance on moral, as opposed to material, sanctions than is common in capitalist countries.

With these preliminaries behind us, it is time to ask why socialists believe that a system of predominantly public ownership and control is superior to a system of predominantly private ownership and control. More specifically, it is time to ask (a) whether socialism eliminates the evils of capitalism and (b) whether socialism generates evils of its own.

First, let us consider unemployment. Socialists argue on theoretical grounds that whereas unemployment is almost inevitable in a capitalist society it is almost impossible in a socialist society. Whether an individual is hired in a capitalist society, they say, depends largely on whether a private employer can make a profit by hiring that individual, and nothing in the capitalist system guarantees the private marketability of everyone's labor power. On the contrary, a large number of unemployed workers—what Marx called an "industrial reserve army"—gives employers a great advantage in dealing with labor. In a socialist society, on the other hand, society itself is the major employer and society can practically always find some use for available labor.

Indeed, the actual employment record of the established socialist countries is good. Not only have they eliminated unemployment as a major social problem; they have generally increased the percentage of the population in the work force. Work is considered not only a right but a duty in socialist countries. There are neither idle rich nor idle poor. Education for socially useful work is made a first priority, and not only for healthy males. Through the use of moral sanctions, the establishment of day-care centers for children, and other means a high percentage of women are recruited into the labor force. And, usually, great efforts are made to educate the mentally and physically handicapped so that they too may assume a useful social role.

What about business cycles? Although business cycles are poorly understood, they have always been widely regarded as a unique feature of capitalism. And, as a matter of fact, they do not exist in any of the established socialist countries. This does not mean, of course, that socialist countries do not have relatively good and bad years. The Soviet Union's rate of economic advance, for example, dipped during World War II with the Nazi invasion. On the whole, however, economic declines have been much fewer and much less severe in socialist than in capitalist countries. More to the point, the ups and downs in socialist countries do not have the characteristic pattern of business cycles in capitalist countries. In bad years there is as a rule little unused industrial capacity and no unemployment. And in good years there is little or no inflation. Whereas recessions and depressions appear to be inherent features of capitalism, bad years in socialist countries are usually due to conditions such as war or drought that have little or nothing to do with the socialist system as such.

This brings us to a more difficult question. In the long run does capitalism or socialism tend to produce the greatest sum of material well-being? Some people seem to think that this question can be answered simply by comparing the actual level of material prosperity in capitalist and socialist countries. But this view is clearly mistaken. Contrary to the expectation of Marx and Engels, socialism came first not to the most industrially advanced countries but to relatively undeveloped countries. A better measure of the performance of capitalist and socialist countries, therefore, is the relative rate of material progress.

But even comparisons of the relative rate of material progress are inconclusive. First, the data on which these comparisons are based are not always complete or reliable. Second, the socialist record is far less extensive than the capitalist record. The Soviet Union, the first of the socialist countries, did not come into existence until 1917. China and the East European countries did not become socialist until the late

1940s. The Castro regime did not come to power in Cuba until 1959. Furthermore, all of the existing socialist nations are governed by Communist parties. Experience with socialism is consequently limited, and it cannot be taken for granted that material progress in emerging or future socialist countries will be at the same rate as in those already established. Third, the record of the capitalist countries differs substantially from one country to another and from one historical period to another. The result is that different comparisons lead to different conclusions. For example, in England and the United States during the nineteenth century the rate of economic progress was generally much higher than it has been at any time in any of the socialist countries. But according to most economists the rate of economic progress in the Soviet Union from 1917 to today has been greater than that of almost any capitalist country over the same period of time. Before World War I Russia ranked low as an industrial power. Today it is second only to the United States.

Finally, and most importantly, the rate of a nation's economic progress cannot be automatically attributed to its economic system. For example, the high rate of economic progress in the Western capitalist countries during the nineteenth century may be due not to capitalism but to the Industrial Revolution and the exploitation of colonies. Similarly, the relatively high rate of economic progress in the Soviet Union may be due not to socialism but to the fact that Russia has been passing through a stage of technological and industrial development comparable to that of the West in the nineteenth century. And, surely, the rate of material progress in a country, like Cuba, that is heavily dependent on the international market price of a single commodity would vary with the market price of that commodity regardless of whether its government were socialist or capitalist.

An informed judgment on this question of productivity, therefore, requires not only close attention to the relative rates of actual material progress, but also careful consideration of various theoretical claims. Socialists argue for the superior productivity of their own system on several grounds.

First, for reasons already explained socialist societies engage a much larger percentage of the population in productive work.

Second, in socialist countries economic progress is not periodically interrupted by recessions or depressions in which much of the usual labor force and existing productive capacity go unused.

Third, socialists claim that some form of overall planning is as necessary for the efficient functioning of a national economy as it is for the success of a large private corporation. But in advanced capitalist countries there is little national economic planning. And in any case the big corporations are always in a position to manipulate whatever national planning commissions may exist for their own selfish purposes. It is worth noting here that according to Marx the combination of an "anarchic" or unregulated national market economy with highly structured and carefully organized private business enterprises constitutes another basic "contradiction" within the capitalist system—which, like the "contradiction" between a public, or collectivized, mode of production and a system of private ownership and management, can only be overcome through socialism.

Fourth, socialists claim that when economic decisions are made by private individuals for private profit rather than by workers' councils and responsible government agencies, there is an enormous waste of natural resources. This claim is echoed by many conservationists and environmentalists throughout the capitalist world.

Finally, socialists argue that they make much better use of human resources. In capitalist societies large numbers of people, often very intelligent and highly educated, are employed in socially useless or even socially detrimental ways: advertising personnel hired to persuade the public to buy items they do not want or need; accountants, lobbyists, and lawyers who spend their entire working lives devising and taking advantage of tax loopholes for the benefit of big corporations and wealthy private individuals; commodity, real estate, and stock market speculators who do nothing but buy and sell in the hope of windfall profits, and so forth. Socialists contend there is no comparable waste in socialist societies.

Those who argue for the superior productivity of capitalism emphasize three theoretical points. First, it is argued that economic planning at the national level is highly inefficient. Human ingenuity is simply not able to cope with the complexities of the economy in a modern industrialized nation.

Second, it is said that although socialist countries employ more persons, they get less work out of them for lack of effective sanctions. By guaranteeing everyone a job and by other excessive welfare measures, socialist societies deprive themselves of the most severe and therefore the most effective negative economic sanctions. At the same time, socialist societies greatly weaken the positive economic sanctions. If an individual plant is controlled democratically by a workers' council, the majority of the workers tend to resent outstanding workers and refuse to give them rewards commensurate with their greater productivity. If, on the other hand, a plant is controlled bureaucratically from the top down, rewards tend to go not to the better worker but to the person who most successfully plays up to superiors. Capitalist owners, who must make a profit or go out of business, can rarely afford to play favorites, but civil servants with nearly absolute job security can and regularly do.

Third, capitalists claim that the goods and services in socialist societies are generally of poor quality and often fail to fit the needs of the intended consumers. To some extent this is attributed to the same lack of effective sanctions that is allegedly responsible for inadequate quantitative outputs. But, capitalists argue, it is primarily due to the lack of an effective market mechanism whereby producers are obliged to take into account the needs and desires of the people. Capitalists, who must have a share of a competitive market to survive, do not rely simply on advertising or packaging to sell their goods. They also do intensive market research not to manipulate desires but rather to discover desires that already exist so as to devise products and services that meet those desires. Members of workers' councils and government bureaucrats, on the other hand, have no incentive to produce goods that are actually desired. Their jobs are secure in any case.

The most crucial arguments against socialism, however, are not economic at all and have nothing to do with material well-being. Rather, they are political and social in nature. Socialism, according to its critics, is a threat to individual rights and democratic institutions. That socialism threatens individual rights is ordinarily said to follow from the fact that socialist governments are bigger and more powerful than those of capitalist societies. From the discussion earlier in this chapter the reader is familiar with the socialist response to the claim that big government is the major threat to individual rights. The socialist response to the related claim that socialism threatens democracy will emerge in the section that follows.

Democracy

For our purposes in this book a social group will be said to be a democracy to the extent that (a) decisions affecting the group are made by a majority of its members and (b) decisions are made after full and free discussion. We shall refer to condition (a) as the principle of *majority rule* and to condition (b) as the principle of *open discussion.*

When all members of a social group are able to participate in the decision-making process both as voters and as advocates, that group is said to practice *pure democracy,* or *direct democracy.* When, on the other hand, the members of a social group take part in the decision-making procedure only indirectly through elected representatives, the group is said to practice *indirect democracy, representative democracy,* or *parliamentary democracy.*

In the large industrial nations of today direct democracy is clearly not possible in the conduct of national affairs. Not only the national government but also national political parties, labor unions, professional associations, religious organizations, and other groups must, if they are to be democratic at all, settle for some form of indirect, or representative, democracy. Even at subnational levels such as the state and the city most democratic organizations are indirect out of necessity. Often, however, some measure of direct democracy is possible at the level of local government. Many New England townships have a system of direct democracy. Relatively direct democracy is also possible in small economic units, local union chapters, residential city block associations, schools, communes, clubs, families, and other small subgroups of the modern industrial nation.

According to many people, especially the student activists of the 1960s, the measure of a modern democratic society is not simply the nature of the political arrangements at the national level but also the extent and effectiveness of direct democracy at those social levels where direct democracy is possible. Advocates of a maximum of direct democracy offer two principal reasons. First, the decisions that most directly affect us are often made by small social groups with whom we are in more or less daily contact, and oppression by these groups can be extremely damaging. This is especially true for the young, who are highly vulnerable to unnecessarily authoritarian or oppressive action in the home and at school. Second, true democratic institutions within larger social groups are relatively rare and are often precarious where they do exist. Unless, therefore, democratic attitudes and habits are learned early and constantly reinforced in the ordinary routines of life, there is no great likelihood that true democracy will prevail within larger social units.

In support of democracy itself, be it direct or indirect, there are three major arguments. First, the only alternative to majority rule is minority rule, and the danger always exists that a minority will abuse its power to promote its own selfish interests at the expense of the majority. Second, the individual who is actively engaged in group decision making and whose voice genuinely counts will as a result be more likely to identify with the group and to accept decisions requiring personal sacrifices for the common good. Third, given that human beings are essentially social animals, those of us who do not participate in the decision making of the social groups to which we belong will have little control over our lives. Instead of being actively involved in shaping our lives, we must passively accept whatever comes. This kind of passivity is incompatible with human dignity.

Despite these impressive arguments few governments anywhere in the world even claimed to be democratic until the French and American Revolutions of the late eighteenth century. The one notable exception was Athens in the fifth century B.C. But in Athens, as in the United States until 1865, democracy coexisted with slavery. And in Athens, as in the United States until 1917, women were not given the right to vote. Moreover, there are two serious criticisms of democratic governments that make even democracy's most enthusiastic champions uneasy.

The Tyranny of the Majority. According to the first major criticism there is no reason to believe that majority governments do any more to promote the welfare of society as a whole than kings, aristocrats, or other minority groups that have held the powers of government. In fact, according to a number of thinkers there is reason to suppose that popular majorities do even less. John Stuart Mill, although he was a staunch supporter of democracy, pointed out that the "tyranny of the majority" can be just as oppressive as the tyranny of a few. As we just saw, powerless minority groups such as slaves have often had to submit to oppression by democratic majorities. And according to Plato and Nietzsche any minority distinguished by intelligence, talent, or moral excellence can expect to be treated shabbily by the majority. For the majority is by definition average or mediocre and will naturally resent those who are superior in any way.

It might be countered here that although majorities may treat minorities badly, at least they will pursue their own interests. And, certainly, it is better that the majority oppress a minority than vice versa. But even the claim that the majority will pursue its own interests has been sharply disputed. Critics of democracy since Plato have repeatedly insisted that the majority has neither the intelligence nor the knowledge to appreciate its own true interests. This argument is often said to be particularly strong in today's highly technological societies where political decisions are apparently even more complex than in the past. Furthermore, even if the majority did know its own interests, the critics say that it could not be expected to act accordingly. The majority, like a child, seeks immediate gratification, not its true well-being. For example, consider that in many poorer countries of the world there is almost no hope of substantial economic development without an immediate sacrifice of consumer goods such as food, clothes, and housing in favor of capital goods such as factories, farm machinery, and schools from which the population can expect to benefit only in the distant future. How many majorities, it is asked, would vote for such sacrifices?

There have been two major responses to this first major criticism of democracy. First, John Stuart Mill and others have argued that democracy can be reconciled with justice for individuals and minority groups by severely limiting the powers of government and consequently the principle of majority rule. If the powers of government are limited and if individuals possess rights that even majority government cannot take away, then of course individuals and minorities are less likely to suffer at the hands of the majority.

Second, Thomas Jefferson and others have argued that the weaknesses of majority rule may be remedied through mass education. For even if the masses cannot be taught to make complex decisions themselves, they can be educated to serve well enough in their role as voters. An educated citizenry, said Jefferson, should be able to recognize and bring to power what Jefferson called an "aristocracy of virtue and talent," by which he meant leaders of broad vision, patriotic sentiments, and a willingness to serve the public interest even at the cost of personal sacrifice. And, although Jefferson himself did not make this point, many later defenders of democracy have insisted that the social issues in modern-day societies are less complex and therefore more easily resolved by persons of modest intelligence and educational attainments than democracy's critics claim. For example, it is clear that the implementation of a national policy favoring public transportation over the private automobile would require a great deal of expertise on the part of specialists in many different areas. But the policy decision itself does not require any expertise. The common sense of the ordinary person, if properly informed, is more than adequate to decide this issue.

Mill's view that a successful democratic society requires (a) severe restrictions on the powers of government and (b) a heavy stress on individual rights is often called "democratic liberalism" (from the Latin word *liber,* meaning free). But since most liberal democrats so defined believe with Jefferson that a successful democratic society also requires (c) mass education and (d) public-spirited leaders, the term democratic liberalism is often used, as we shall be using it here, to refer to a view that emphasizes all four of these factors. (It should be noted that this usage of the term "liberalism" differs from the more popular twentieth-century usage according to which liberalism occupies a position to the left of center on a political spectrum. The British Liberal Party, which draws its inspiration from John Stuart Mill, is right of center in British politics.)

Factionalism. The second major criticism of democracy also goes back to Plato. In the twentieth century it has been most often voiced by fascists such as Mussolini and Hitler. According to this criticism, in the absence of a strong leader or elite group with dictatorial powers society breaks up into many different centers of power, conflicting interest groups, or factions—each of which is single-mindedly dedicated to its own goals without regard for the common good. Democracy, therefore, means chronic instability and neglect of basic national problems. In effect, this criticism denies the practicability of Jefferson's ideal of an enlightened public supporting able, public-minded leaders. The criticism presupposes that democratic politics is essentially a struggle among numerous and inherently amoral power groups, whose antagonisms and power plays are profoundly divisive unless curbed by a strong dictatorial regime.

The usual response to this second major criticism of democracy is made from the standpoint of a position sometimes called *democratic pluralism.* The democratic pluralists do not deny a substantial measure of truth in the criticism. Rather, they tend to make a virtue out of the alleged weaknesses. They agree that the democratic political struggle is basically an amoral contest among many different groups with conflicting interests and little concern for the common good. They also agree that the result of the democratic process is a series of uneasy compromises—punctuated by intermittent crises—among those various interest groups. But, they say, the compromises achieved by the democratic process tend to represent the true balance of power among the contenders, since in a democracy every group is equally free to organize and to make its political weight felt. And, as the fascists rightly see, the only alternative to the free play of opposing forces within the context of representative democracy is a military dictatorship. For the democratic pluralists, therefore, a degree of instability and the absence of clear overall directions in national policy is the price that must be paid for freedom.

For some time most democrats on the European continent have held to some version of democratic pluralism. And today many former liberal democrats in England and America have come to defend democracy in essentially the same way as the democratic pluralists. Increasingly, democracy is being viewed as a very imperfect form of government that is to be defended less by pointing to its virtues than by pointing to the shortcomings of alternative forms of government.

Important though the problems associated with these two traditional criticisms of democracy are, there is another equally pressing problem with regard to democracy. This problem has been raised by the Marxists and has to do with the impact of a capitalist economy on democratic institutions. The Marxists do not quarrel with the principles of free discussion and majority rule. On the contrary, they profess a firm devotion to these principles. But, they claim, democratic ideals cannot be realized in a capitalist society, or even in a socialist society so long as it is surrounded by hostile capitalist nations. In a capitalist world, they say, democratic institutions, which in theory permit the majority to promote its own welfare, are inevitably subverted and in practice serve the interests of a small minority at the expense of the substantial majority.

Like the democratic pluralists, the Marxists see the political process as essentially a struggle of irreconcilable interest groups. But the Marxists contest the democratic pluralists' contention that the participants in this power struggle are a miscellaneous group of various centers of power whose representation in the political process is roughly proportional to their numbers. As the Marxists see it, in a capitalist society there are only two major antagonists: (a) the *bourgeoisie,* or *capitalist class,* a small group that owns and manages the means of production for private profit, and (b) the *proletariat,* or *working class,* a large group that is exploited, or forced to sell its labor power for less than the value of its output. And in the struggle between these two classes the bourgeoisie is said to possess all of the tactical advantages except numbers.

Marxists believe that the superior economic power of the capitalists permits them to manipulate the democratic process to their own advantage at every turn. The principle of majority rule is undermined because in capitalist societies candidates for public office cannot run effectively without spending huge sums of money. This means that working-class candidates will be screened out early in the electoral process. If, by chance, a few are elected, they can be bought off or intimidated once in office. Similarly, Marxists argue that the principle of free discussion is undermined because in capitalist countries the "free press" and other media are hardly more than propaganda instruments of the capitalist class. Persons who genuinely represent the interests of the workers have wholly inadequate access to the media. Thus, representative, or parliamentary, democracy under capitalism is in fact a disguised *dictatorship of the bourgeoisie,* by which Marxists mean not a military dictatorship but rather effective political rule by a minority class.

As noted earlier, the Marxists' criticism of democracy under capitalism is not a criticism of democracy as such. In fact, their criticism is accompanied by a plan for overcoming class divisions and ushering in a society in which democracy may truly flourish. Traditionally, two steps were envisaged. The first was an armed revolutionary overthrow of the bourgeois dictatorship. Socialist forces that attempt to come to power through democratic parliamentary procedures will, it was said, find victory snatched from their grasp. The national bourgeoisie and its foreign allies will use any means, including illegal sabotage, political assassination, and military rebellion, to maintain their privileges. As evidence for this claim traditional Marxists often point to the history of the Spanish Republic in the 1930s and of the Allende regime in Chile in the early 1970s. In both cases legally elected socialist governments were violently overthrown by capitalist forces that instituted military dictatorships to maintain power.

The second step traditionally envisaged was a temporary, or transitional, *dictatorship of the proletariat,* or effective political rule by the majority. This must be maintained until the national bourgeoisie and its foreign allies are no longer a threat. Once the prerevolutionary domestic capitalist powers are destroyed and once subversion or invasion by external capitalist enemies is no longer feared, the dictatorship of the proletariat will be relaxed. And in time the state itself—defined as the branch of government with effective control over police and military power—will "wither away." Of the transitional government apparatus nothing will remain but democratically elected agencies charged exclusively with the "administration of things" rather than the "domination of persons." These agencies will rule exclusively by the force of moral authority. As evidence of the need for a temporary dictatorship of the proletariat, traditional Marxists often point to the invasion of the Soviet Union by the Western Powers shortly after the Revolution and the United States' sponsored invasion of Cuba at the Bay of Pigs in 1961.

In rejoinder democratic capitalists make two major points. First, it is said that if the bourgeoisie had as tight a control over the democratic process as the Marxists claim, it would be hard to explain (a) why welfare capitalism has almost everywhere triumphed over laissez-faire capitalism despite the opposition by the bourgeoisie and (b) why Socialist and even Communist parties have gained the substantial support they enjoy today in capitalist countries such as France, Italy, and Japan. Second, it is argued that the revolutionary remedy to excessive bourgeois control over the political process is worse than the ailment itself. As Marxists agree, a violent revolution is an evil that can be justified only by its results. But the classless society and the withering away of the state are said to be utopian pipe dreams. No dictatorship once established has ever voluntarily yielded power. And none ever will, because the drives for power and economic advantage are deeply rooted in human nature. Moreover, it is said that a socialist dictatorship would be even more difficult to dislodge than a right-wing dictatorship, since a socialist government has far more power by virtue of its control over the economy as well as over the police and the military. A democratic capitalist society, despite its imperfections, is said to be the only kind of society in which power is sufficiently dispersed to give the individual some breathing room.

Significantly, most Marxist groups in the industrialized democratic nations—including the Communist parties of France, Italy, and Japan—have been moving away from the traditional Marxist view with regard to violent revolution and a dictatorship of the proletariat. One reason for this trend is the success of the Soviet Revolution. The Soviet Union's present status as an established socialist superpower considerably reduces the danger that a socialist electoral triumph would be subverted by an alliance between the local bourgeoisie and its foreign allies. Capitalist countries would think twice before risking a military confrontation with Russia.

A second reason for this movement away from the traditional Marxist position is the failure of the Soviet Union to liberalize substantially its own political regime as the danger of domestic and foreign subversion has faded. Despite a basic sense of fraternity with the Soviet Union, or at least an acute awareness of an eventual need for its help and protection, many Socialist and even Communist parties have become increasingly critical of Soviet political institutions. The continued denial of individual rights and the continued heavily centralized control by the national state and the Party apparatus so many years after the Revolution tend to confirm the claim that dictatorships do not easily wither away.

Finally, experience since the Soviet Revolution in 1917 shows that there is more than one road to socialism, and that the pattern of political and economic development under a socialist regime owes much to a country's national heritage and special circumstances. Accordingly, most socialists today are less rigid and doctrinaire than in the past. In particular, socialists in the industrialized, democratic nations today are well aware of the differences between their own situations and those of the pioneer socialist countries. As already noted, if one of these nations chose to go socialist today, it would be less isolated internationally. The new socialist government would also, of course, have a much stronger economic base and much stronger democratic traditions on which to build. Unlike its socialist predecessors in Russia, China, and Cuba, it would not have to cope with extreme poverty, widespread illiteracy, and an historical legacy of authoritarian government. Nor would it have to impose upon the masses a heavy sacrifice of consumer goods for the sake of rapid industrialization or to maintain an exceptionally costly military establishment in order to protect its right to exist.

Notwithstanding these developments it is still difficult to predict the reactions of capitalist powers to another socialist electoral triumph or to gauge the depth and sincerity of recently professed commitments by several European Communist Parties to a nonrevolutionary and democratic transition to socialism. Many critics regard these public statements as deceitful tactical maneuvers.

Chapter 4

Good
Character

The value attributed to any given character trait varies from one historical epoch to another. For example, in ancient Greece and Rome physical courage was prized far more than it generally is today. Similarly, in medieval Europe obedience and humility were more highly regarded than they are today. Differences also exist from one society to another within the same historical epoch and within a single society at any one time. In capitalist societies competitiveness is generally valued more than in socialist societies. But within any contemporary society, be it capitalist or socialist, there are significant differences of opinion regarding the importance of competitiveness.

To some extent these differences reflect disagreements with respect to the nature of the good life and the good society. For instance, the medieval emphasis on obedience and humility probably followed from the heavy medieval emphasis on stability as a social ideal. To some extent these differences reflect disagreements concerning the social consequences of a given character trait. For example, the capitalist emphasis on competitiveness tends to go with the conviction that competitiveness is highly productive. Finally, differing evaluations of a character trait often reflect a just appreciation of differing objective historical circumstances. For example, in ancient Greece and Rome, where military combat normally took the form of face-to-face fighting, physical bravery had a greater social utility than in contemporary societies, where military success depends more on skill in the use of technologically sophisticated weapons.

In what follows our concern is principally with character traits that are widely believed to be important in modern-day industrial societies. The reader will notice, however, that many of these traits are clearly essential to successful social living no matter what the circumstances may be.

Rationality

In Chapter Two we defined rationality as a set of dispositions (practices, habits, tendencies) that permit us (a) to increase our knowledge and (b) to extend the range of behavior in which proper deliberation and due regard for our best all-round, long-term interests play a proper role. Alternatively, rationality may be defined in terms of dispositions that tend to result in wise and effective decisions in matters of practical importance. Given either of these definitions, rationality must be distinguished from mere curiosity, simple logicality, or ivory-tower intellectualism. On our use of the term, "rationality" is much closer to what philosophers in the past have called "wisdom" or "practical reason."

The more concrete definition that follows consists of a list of six dispositions that normally characterize the rational person:

1. A basic mark of the rational person is the tendency to seek out whatever relevant information is available before acting in matters of practical concern. It is irrational to choose a career without knowledge of the available options and of one's own abilities and shortcomings. It is no less irrational to vote for a candidate for public office without a knowledge of the candidate's background and program.

2. Another basic mark of the rational person is respect for the norms of logic in interpreting whatever factual data are available. The rational person, for example, habitually asks whether the interpretation that first comes to mind is consistent with all the facts, whether there are other interpretations consistent with the facts, and if so whether a way of testing the rival interpretations exists.

3. A rational person regularly seeks to discover and to keep in check all of those factors that tend to warp judgment. The rational person, for example, is acutely aware of the human tendency to believe what one wishes to be true, to think well of friends and ill of enemies, to accept uncritically the views that prevail in one's own society, and to believe that a policy favoring one's own interests is just and a policy damaging to one's interests unjust. It has been said that humankind

is not a rational animal but rather an *intermittently* rational animal. The validity of this remark is never more apparent than when one reviews the many basic human dispositions that dispose us to biased and prejudiced opinions.

4. Rational persons proportion the strength of their convictions to the strength of the evidence, reserving judgment entirely where the evidence gives no warrant for belief. Consequently, they retain open minds with regard to the reasonable opinions of others and are willing to reexamine their own views whenever fresh evidence becomes available. In short, rational persons reject dogmatism in all of its forms.

5. Rational persons will frequently submit their views on controversial issues of importance to the criticism of intelligent and informed critics, or opponents. For, as anyone who has tried to live up to the ideals implicit in points (1) through (4) will have learned, the criticism of those who disagree with us is by far the most valuable source of overlooked but relevant factual data and by far the most effective protection against erroneous inferences, personal biases, and undue certainty.

6. Finally, rational persons do all in their power to implement the decisions arrived at through the five practices enumerated. For example, rational persons resist the temptation to succumb to immediate gratification and accept whatever short-run costs or sacrifices reason may require. They also accept the temporary psychological discomfort and insecurity that normally attend the critical examination of cherished beliefs and the discipline of maintaining an open mind.

As we noted in Chapter Two, rationality is a trait from which society greatly profits, since much antisocial behavior is irrational. For example, criminologists generally agree that a high percentage of crimes are irrational. As we also saw in Chapter Two, any society that hopes to introduce an effective set of sanctions must assume a substantial measure of rationality among those whose behavior the sanctions are designed to affect. Since sanctions work by appealing to self-interest, persons who have no rational regard for self-interest are not motivated by them.

Moreover, widespread individual rationality is a necessary condition of social stability. The reason for this is that in any given situation there are ordinarily countless irrational courses of behavior but few rational ones. If, therefore, individuals cannot be counted on to behave rationally, their behavior cannot be predicted with any reasonable degree of reliability. And, as we saw in Chapter Two, predictability is the essence of stability. Thus, Adam Smith, Karl Marx, and virtually every other economist has regularly assumed that individuals and groups not only pursue their own economic self-interests but on the whole do so rationally. Without this assumption of rationality it appears to be impossible to construct any economic theory with the slightest predictive power.

Finally, human beings constantly try to dress up their own self-interests and their own socially inherited prejudices with moral finery. The tendency to seek a moral justification for unjust and selfish behavior is one of the most deep-seated and insidious traits of the human species. And there is absolutely no effective remedy for this tendency except countertendencies formed through the habitual practice of rationality.

Despite its vast social importance rationality has rarely been sufficiently appreciated, and almost no society has seriously used moral or other sanctions to encourage it. In fact, many societies have seriously downgraded rationality or even treated it with outright hostility.

One reason that rationality has not been fully appreciated derives from its being primarily a self-regarding virtue—that is, a character trait that individuals normally cultivate with a view to their own benefit. By contrast the virtue of benevolence is an *other-regarding virtue*—that is, a virtue practiced with a view toward the welfare of others. If one is benevolent, then by definition one cares about the welfare of others and consciously works for their benefit. There is nothing in the definition of rationality, however, that requires the rational agent to take the welfare of others into account.

Clearly, the distinction between self-regarding and other-regarding virtues has merit, and it is undeniable that rationality is primarily a self-regarding virtue. But difficulties arise when it is assumed that other-regarding virtues must be socially more advantageous than rationality. This inference is unwarranted for several reasons. First, the social utility of a character trait has to do with its consequences, not with what is going on in the mind of the agent at the moment of action. And there is no necessary connection between intention or motive and result. For reasons already pointed out, purely self-regarding rational behavior often has very desirable social results.

Second, although nothing in the definition of rationality requires rational behavior to be other-regarding, nothing in the definition of rationality prevents rational behavior from being other-regarding. On the contrary, if a rational person is also benevolent, self-interest itself requires a rational effort to promote the welfare of others. For instance, if a parent's happiness depends on the happiness of the children, then the parent must, if rational, work for their happiness.

Finally, although other-regarding virtues play an important and indisputable role in the morally good life, they have little value unless accompanied and guided by rationality. For example, no matter how much parents may love their children, their love is worth little unless they are sufficiently rational to work effectively for the children's benefit. Indeed, many children have been greatly damaged by overindulgent parents who lacked wisdom and understanding. Consider also, the heretics and witches tortured or burned at the stake because of someone's misguided sense of duty. The simple truth is that the value of all virtues, be they other-regarding or self-regarding, depends on their being informed with reason. Rationality is not only a virtue in its own right. It is also an indispensable condition for the proper exercise of all other virtues.

Another major reason that rationality has not been given its full due derives from a fairly widespread belief that it poses a threat to social stability and social cohesion. These social goals, it is said, depend on widespread dedication to a set of traditional beliefs and ideals, and this dedication is impossible when reason usurps the role of tradition. There is a profound suspicion of the tendency of rational individuals to subject all of their beliefs, including those in which they were indoctrinated as children, to critical examination. There is also great impatience with the open-mindedness of rational persons, their willingness to admit that the beliefs by which their society lives may be subject to criticism and their willingness to entertain the possibility that the beliefs of those their society considers enemies may have some rational foundation.

There are, however, many persuasive arguments against the contention that rationality threatens social stability and cohesion. First, as we saw in Chapter Two, many people feel that stability and social cohesion should be based on widespread participation in the political process and a common dedication to future goals. For them the suspicion that rationality undermines stability and cohesion betrays an undue emphasis on passively acquired traditional ideals and the chauvinistic ingroup-outgroup mentality.

Second, even if one grants the social importance of a common devotion to traditional ideals, there is much to be said for John Stuart

Mill's contention that traditional beliefs lose their force and vitality unless periodically challenged. If Mill is right on this point, attacks on social tradition by critical and open-minded persons are not an impediment to but rather an important condition of that tradition's vitality. The nineteenth-century Danish existentialist philosopher Sören Kierkegaard, made the same point more concretely with respect to the Christian tradition. He said that if being a Christian is merely a matter of being born in a Christian country, going to church on Sundays, and mechanically repeating certain religious formulas, then the Christian tradition for all practical purposes is dead. According to Kierkegaard, the militant atheist, who at least cares enough about the tradition to attack it, is actually closer to being a Christian than the conventional "believer."

Third, granting again the importance of tradition to social stability and cohesion, one must ask whether respect for tradition should be blind, or irrational. If every generation inherits much of value from preceding generations, it also inherits a fairly large share of prejudices and injustices. Furthermore, every new generation faces challenges posed by changing historical circumstances. And who but a rational person could distinguish between the good and the bad, the just and the unjust, the useful and the outmoded traditions.

Finally, if a major part of a country's tradition is a widely shared belief in mutual tolerance and respect for individual and group differences, rationality cannot be a great threat to the vitality of that tradition. And if a country's traditions do not include a commitment to tolerance and diversity, it may be time to alter the traditional base on which that society rests.

Conformity and Individuality

As we have several times pointed out, in order to secure major goals such as harmony and stability, society must create an environment that positively sanctions socially desirable behavior and negatively sanctions socially undesirable behavior. Criminals must be punished. Energetic and productive citizens must be rewarded. Lazy and non-productive citizens must be penalized. And so forth. Moreover, as we saw in the last section, the effectiveness of the external social sanctions depends by and large upon individuals' concern for their own rational, or enlightened, self-interest. No character trait of special moral significance other than rationality is normally required.

Certain external social sanctions, however, become effective only if an additional character trait of special social significance is present. These are the moral sanctions—praise and blame or other means by which society communicates to the individual its approval or disapproval of various forms of conduct. For these moral sanctions to be effective it is not enough that those for whom they are designed be rational. It is also necessary that they have some measure of what we shall call *conformity*—that is, a disposition to experience intrinsic satisfaction when their behavior is socially approved and to experience intrinsic dissatisfaction when their behavior is disapproved. People lacking in conformity are often called "shameless."

For reasons that will be explained shortly, conformity is often excessive. In fact, some philosophers—most notably Kant—have denied that it has any moral value whatsoever. And most moral philosophers have placed it low on their list of virtues. Nonetheless, it seems to be an inescapable fact that concern for the good opinion of others plays a greater role in producing an acceptable minimal level of moral behavior among most human beings than any single character trait except rationality. And there is good reason to believe that other desirable character traits—especially conscientiousness, which Kant considered the only character trait with genuine moral value—could not develop at all in persons to whom conformity is unknown. The American social critic H. L. Mencken was unduly cynical when he said a bad conscience is merely a feeling that somebody is looking over one's shoulder. But there is general agreement, as we shall see later, that the sense of duty, at least in good part, grows out of originally conformist attitudes.

There are still people who believe that the moral education of the young should be principally a matter of strict discipline enforced with physical sanctions such as a belt and a supper of bread and water. But the general superiority of moral sanctions as an instrument of socialization is today not only widely recognized by the public but also supported by a considerable body of psychological research. Even among adults it is difficult to think of any sanctions that have as pervasive and profound an influence. In an office or professional association a snub often creates worse personnel problems than a grave injury or injustice. For most people a term in prison is in itself far less serious than the shame or odium that accompanies a prison record. There is hardly a country in the world in which slander is not a recognized crime with heavy penalties. As Shakespeare wrote: "Who steals my purse steals trash. . . . But he that filches from me my good name . . . makes me poor indeed." (*Othello*, III. 1.)

The near universality and depth of the conformist disposition is easily understood in view of humankind's pervasive sociality and the threat represented to each of us by the indifference or hostility of others. There is, therefore, little danger that ordinary human beings will be insufficiently conformist. The more common danger, as most traditional philosophers have pointed out, is that the individual conform to excess. For the same conformist tendency that makes it possible to teach and to maintain minimal standards of honesty or fairness is also responsible for perpetuating evils like witch-hunting, slavery, sexism, and racism. As long as one's sole or principal aim is to be well thought of and to reduce the threat posed by the indifference or hostility of others, one will conform to whatever social standards happen to prevail without regard to the moral merits or demerits of those standards. And one will tend irrationally not only to repress any serious questions about those standards but also to resent those who do raise such questions. In other words, the more one tends to conform, the greater the danger that one will put excessive faith in what Plato called "the opinion of the many" and insufficient faith in one's own rational powers and one's own moral conscience. In still other words, conformity is usually at odds with the moral courage required to stand alone or with a minority against a disapproving majority.

Thus, although conformity is an indispensable and major incentive to morally good conduct, it has a natural tendency to become excessive and must be countered by a second character trait that we shall call *individuality*. By this we mean precisely the disposition to stand alone or with a minority whenever reason or conscience requires. The social value of individuality will be obvious to everyone who fully appreciates the extent to which the views and standards that prevail in any society are a product of traditional prejudices, the propaganda of powerful self-interested minorities, and sheer ignorance or intellectual laziness.

In addition to the conformist tendency to inhibit individuality there is a second reason for the traditional suspicion of conformity. As has been frequently pointed out, general social approval often goes not to the genuinely good person but to the person who merely appears to be good. In other words, the external moral sanctions combined with conformity are not reliable incentives to good conduct; often, they are merely an invitation to hypocrisy. And for this reason, too, traditional moral philosophers have downgraded conformity in favor of the more reliable internal moral sanctions to which we now turn.

Conscientiousness

Morally conscientious people, it will be recalled, suffer from a sense of guilt, or bad conscience, when they act in ways that they consider morally undesirable. They also experience a sense of personal worth, or self-respect, when they believe they have behaved well in a morally trying situation. A well-developed conscience, or strong sense of duty, however, has several additional features that help to define it and to explain why it has such a special "feel."

First, conscience is highly self-conscious. To experience the pangs of bad conscience, or the sense of guilt, one must be able to form an image of oneself as one actually is, to form an image of oneself as one would like to be, and to perceive the gap between these two images. Similarly, to experience the satisfaction of a good conscience, or the sense of one's own moral worth, one must be able to contrast an image of oneself as one actually is and wants to be with an image of oneself as one would be were it not for one's sense of duty. If there is no ideal self-image, there can be no conscience.

By itself, however, the possession of an ideal self-image is not enough. A football player, for example, might have a clear image of the kind of player he would like to be and of his shortcomings relative to that image without experiencing a bad conscience. Similarly, professional thieves might see themselves as bunglers in the light of certain exacting standards that they set for themselves, but they would not for this reason be said to suffer from a bad conscience. Also required—and this is the second major feature of conscience—is an ideal self-image that bids us adhere to rules or principles with social value. The person whose self-image requires adherence to rules such as truth telling and promise keeping has a moral conscience. The achievement-oriented person whose self-image merely requires expertise in the execution of personal goals does not.

Third, the conscientious person has a regard for consistency, or impartiality, in the application of rules. This does not mean that moral rules must be followed blindly without regard to special circumstances. If we had to break a promise to save someone's life, most of us could conscientiously break the rule of promise keeping. Consistency, or impartiality, in the application of rules does mean, however, that we must not make exceptions for ourselves unless we are willing to make exceptions for others under the same circumstances. Thus, the ideal self-image of the conscientious person requires not only adherence to rules with a social value but also a sense of oneself as a member of a community in which one is an equal without special rights or privileges.

Finally, even when the rules conscience urges us to follow are the same as the rules society directs us to obey, the satisfaction accompanying a good conscience is different from the satisfaction of knowing that one's behavior is socially approved. Similarly, the pangs of bad conscience are different from the pain or discomfort of knowing that one is badly thought of by others. The external moral sanctions may be experienced in the absence of the internal sanctions and vice versa. Moreover, one set of sanctions may be favorable while the other is unfavorable. That is, one may have a good conscience with regard to an action that is socially disapproved or a bad conscience with regard to an action that is socially approved. Many moral and social reformers, for example, have claimed that it was only the sense of personal dignity and self-worth accompanying a good conscience that sustained them in the face of public hostility. Plato put it more poetically when he had Socrates say in *Gorgias:* "I would rather that my lyre should be inharmonious, and that there be no music in the chorus which I provided: aye, or that the whole world should be at odds with me, and oppose me, rather than that I myself should be at odds with myself. . . ."

Unlike conformity, a nearly universal trait that is easily understood, conscientiousness is by no means universal and it is still poorly understood. In some cultures it hardly exists at all. Even in cultures where it is most widespread, it is only partially developed or distorted in substantial segments of the population.

In the twentieth century the most popular account of conscience derives from Freud. Like many other thinkers, Freud was struck by the general similarity between the dictates of individual conscience and the dictates of parents or society. He assumed, therefore, that conscience is an "internalization" of parental or social commands. But, why is it, Freud asked, that the strength of conscience varies so greatly from one person to another? Why should some people be almost indescribably tortured by feelings of guilt whereas others hardly know what guilt is? Freud's answer was as follows: By birth all of us have a certain sum of energy that would normally be expended in aggressive or destructive behavior. Originally, this energy is directed against those who frustrate our search for personal gratification. But since aggression with an external focus often invites punishment or retaliation, a part of the aggressive energy is often diverted from its original object, attaches to conscience—in Freudian vocabulary the "superego"—and is redirected against the self. In other words, the force of conscience depends on how much of the aggressive energy we are born with is turned inward in the form of self-aggression, or self-punishment.

In support of his theory Freud tells us that the saints, who suffer most from feelings of guilt, are the least aggressive in their dealings with others, whereas hardened criminals, who as a rule do not suffer at all from conscience, are the most aggressive. And although Freud did not make this point, later supporters of his theory have observed that there is generally an inverse correlation between homicide, or the killing of others, and suicide, or the killing of self. In populations with a high rate of homicide—for example, among Catholics and the young —there is usually a low rate of suicide. Conversely, in populations with a high rate of suicide—for example, Protestants and the elderly —there is usually a low rate of homicide.

There are, however, several weaknesses in Freud's theory. First, it is very difficult to substantiate the assumption of an inborn aggressive drive. Second, the evidence for an inverse correlation between externally directed aggression and guilt is far from conclusive. The psychology of sainthood and criminality is inadequately understood to say the least, and conclusions based on generalizations with regard to saints and hardened criminals must be treated with caution. The data on homicide and suicide must also be carefully examined. Although the inverse correlation between homicide and suicide does generally hold, there are many notable exceptions. The English, for example, have a low homicide and a low suicide rate, whereas the Americans have a high homicide and a high suicide rate. Moreover, ordinary people almost unanimously report that it is precisely aggressive behavior toward others that most regularly and forcefully triggers guilt feelings. Third, Freud's theory does not give any explanation for good conscience. Perhaps good conscience is merely the absence of bad conscience, a sense of relief at not being tortured by feelings of guilt. But this explanation does not fit most descriptions of good conscience.

What appears to be involved in good conscience is not merely relief from guilt, but a strong, positive sense of worth, or pride. Fourth, Freud's theory does not explain why, as in the case of many moral reformers, the dictates of individual conscience do not always duplicate the dictates of parents and society nor why some individuals actually oppose parents and society in the name of conscience. Finally, Freud's theory gives no clue as to why consistency and impartiality play so important a role in the thinking of people with a highly developed conscience.

Fortunately, there is a second twentieth-century theory of conscience, developed by the Swiss-French psychologist Jean Piaget, that makes up for most of the weaknesses in Freud's theory. Piaget, like Freud, duly noted that most individuals subscribe to the moral rules of their parents or society, and like Freud he felt that this could best be explained by assuming some process of internalization. In the moral development of children conscience is at first merely an internalization of parental or social authority, and children accept the internalized authority because they experience it as a substitute parent with a similar role as punisher. But, according to Piaget, this early conscience, which he calls the *authoritarian conscience,* is only an immature form of conscience, which should be and normally is transformed into a more mature form of conscience, which he calls the *autonomous conscience* (self-governing conscience).

The development of the mature, or autonomous, conscience occurs not in early childhood but rather in late childhood and early adolescence. The social setting is not the family or parent-child relationship but the peer group, or group of equals (other children in the classroom or on the playground, for example). And the chief characteristic of the mature conscience is not an internalization of the authoritarian parent-child relationship based on fear and punishment. Rather, it is a sense of self as a full-fledged and equal member of a community that lives by rules of its own making. The individual who obeys these rules also legislates them and obeys them precisely for this reason. To violate the rules would be not only to break faith with one's community but to break faith with one's self, to violate a self-imposed commitment. It is for this reason that the conscience formed through peer-group activities is called autonomous rather than authoritarian.

Hardly less important than peer-group activities to the formation of the autonomous conscience is the intellectual development of the individual. For it is only as the child comes to appreciate elementary logical principles—especially the principle of logical consistency, or noncontradiction—that the child can appreciate the moral principle of impartiality. And it is by reference to the logical, or intellectual, conscience with its demands for consistency that we can best understand moral reformers, or persons who in the name of morality reject one or more of the conventional moral rules in which their society has indoctrinated them. Consider, for example, the antiracist in a racist society. Since a racist society, like any society that is capable of surviving at all, must have some commitment to the principle of justice and since rules governing the relationship between the races in a racist society conflict with the principle of justice, we can understand the antiracist as someone who is affronted by logical inconsistencies. If we reject this analysis of the moral reformers' motivation, we seem to be obliged to regard moral reformers as seers who pick their unconventional rules out of thin air.

Piaget, who was trained as a philosopher before turning to psychology, is heavily indebted to Kant, from whom he derived the notion that a sound moral conscience must be autonomous and that maturely conscientious persons would abide only by rules of their own making. In Kantian terminology the immature, or authoritarian, conscience is *heteronomous*—that is, its source lies outside the individual. From Kant Piaget also derived the idea that the intellectual and the moral conscience are closely linked. But Piaget is best known for extensive and detailed studies with children in which he tried to show how the mature conscience develops. And under his inspiration, a great deal of psychological research on the nature of conscience is now under way in the United States. (The best-known name in this connection is that of Lawrence Kohlberg.) It is still too early to say whether this research will confirm Piaget's belief in the importance of the peer group to the formation of mature conscience. But already there is an impressive body of evidence in support of a link between intellectual conscience and moral conscience.

Benevolence

The reader will recall from Chapter Two that *benevolence* is a disposition, or tendency, for a person to be personally pleased by the happiness of others and to be personally pained by the unhappiness of others. In other words, benevolence has to do with what we feel on noting the joy or suffering of others. To the extent that we are benevolent we delight in the company of happy people. Their happiness tends to transmit itself to us. At the same time to the extent that we are benevolent we are uncomfortable, depressed, or upset when confronted with the suffering of others. The spectacle of their suffering causes us to suffer as well. This second aspect of benevolence is called "compassion." The opposites of benevolence are *indifference,* an unemotional detachment from others, or *malevolence,* a tendency to be personally pained by the happiness of others and personally pleased by their unhappiness.

The social utility of benevolence, especially if deeply engrained and widespread, is clear. Benevolent persons are much more inclined than indifferent or malevolent persons to promote the interests of others, since by so doing they contribute to their own well-being. Feelings of benevolence operate as sanctions, socializing individuals by rewarding them for socially valuable behavior and punishing them for socially undesirable behavior. And, as we noted earlier in this chapter, internal sanctions such as conscientiousness and benevolence are more reliable than external moral sanctions. For whereas the good opinion of others may be acquired by deceit or hypocrisy, the rewards of conscientiousness and benevolence may not.

The concept of benevolence is related to the concept of unselfishness, and in some everyday contexts "benevolence" and "unselfishness" are used synonymously. The term "unselfishness," however, is often used more loosely and broadly than the term "benevolence." For example, individuals who give to charities or other causes out of a sense of duty might be said to be unselfish even though they are indifferent to the welfare of those who benefit from their giving and cannot therefore be called benevolent.

Also, for many people the term "unselfishness" strongly suggests self-sacrifice on the part of the agent. In fact, there are those who say that the person who derives any form of personal reward, or compensation, from behavior promoting the interests of others is acting selfishly. But, as we are using the term "benevolent," people who act benevolently do derive a personal reward from their benevolence— namely, the satisfaction of relieving the pain they personally experience when others suffer or of enjoying the pleasure they personally experience when others are happy. Those who refuse to call behavior that brings a personal reward to the agent unselfish apparently believe that people who advance the interests of others without any gain for themselves are morally superior to those who help themselves while helping others. They alone, therefore, are entitled to be called unselfish. As we shall see in Chapter Six, this view appears to rest on a confusion. In any case, the concept of benevolence as defined here directs our attention to a pressing social problem: How can we encourage people to respond to the well-being or unhappiness of others with the same kind of emotional concern evoked by their own good or bad fortune?

According to one view, advanced by the eighteenth-century British philosopher David Hume and some of his contemporaries, benevolence is an inborn trait of humankind, a part of human nature. We take a sympathetic, emotionally involved interest in the welfare of others simply because it is in our nature to do so. Benevolence is an instinct. Unfortunately those who have taken this view have not said whether benevolence is a rigid instinct like the blinking reflex or a more plastic instinct like hunger or sexuality. And this is a matter of some importance. For if benevolence is a rigid instinct, then society is powerless to promote or inhibit its exercise. If, however, benevolence is a plastic instinct, then presumably society can play a role in promoting or inhibiting its exercise. It is probably safe to assume, however, that those who speak of "natural" benevolence take instincts such as hunger and sexuality rather than instincts such as the blinking reflex as their model. For, clearly, benevolence like sexuality admits of greater and lesser degrees. Just as some persons have a stronger sex drive than others, so some are more benevolent than others. Also, benevolence, like sexuality, can be countered by other drives or needs. Just as we are often ambivalent toward others as sex objects, we are often ambivalent toward others in nonsexual ways. We wish them well and wish them ill at the same time.

It would appear, however, that if benevolence is rooted in our instinctual nature at all, its roots are less profound than the roots of hunger or sexuality. In most societies most people do have moderately strong benevolent feelings toward at least a few persons, but benevolence is neither so universal nor so strong as the sexual appetite. In some societies indifference and malevolence are the rule rather than the exception, and in a few societies benevolence even toward family members is practically unknown. It must be concluded, therefore, that social circumstances play a greater role in the development of benevolence than in the development of sexuality and other highly instinctual forms of behavior.

What, then, are the social circumstances that account for the development and strength of benevolent feelings? To this question two different but not incompatible answers have been proposed. According to one answer benevolence is nurtured in early life by a set of circumstances that condition children to associate the well-being of others with their own personal well-being. According to the second answer benevolence is a product of group identification. We shall examine each of these views in turn.

The concept of social conditioning grew out of a set of famous experiments by the Russian psychologist and physiologist Ivan Pavlov. In these experiments a group of dogs, who normally salivate at the sight of food, were repeatedly presented with food to the accompaniment of a ringing bell. Eventually the bell was rung in the absence of food, and it was observed that the dogs responded to the bell by salivating just as they had earlier responded to food. In like manner, it is said, children learn early that when a parent or another important person in their lives is in a good humor, they are the recipients of favors and gifts that give them pleasure. At the same time children notice that they are often subject to deprivation or ill-treatment when their parents or other significant persons are upset or unhappy. The result is that over time children come to associate the well-being of others with their own personal well-being and the unhappiness of others with personal unhappiness. Moreover, this association is stronger than the association of a bell with food made by Pavlov's dogs, because the link between the child's well-being and the well-being of others is causal and the child, being intelligent, realizes this. The well-being of others is not just accidentally associated with personal well-being; it is a means to personal well-being. In the language of Chapter One, the well-being of others is originally an instrumental good, and like all instrumental goods that are not positively disagreeable to the agent there is a tendency for them to become in time intrinsic goods.

This explanation of benevolence is supported by evidence indicating that where the normal link between the well-being of others and personal well-being is absent, the child tends to grow up indifferent to the welfare of others. Children reared in orphanages where the treatment is perfunctory and impersonal are said to grow up with severely limited capabilities for emotional involvement in the lives of others. The explanation is also strengthened by evidence indicating that malevolence is greatly promoted when children grow up believing that their parents have deprived them in favor of other offspring. In order to prevent the development of a generalized sense of hostility to others psychologists recommend among other things that on the occasion of one child's birthday all the children in the family be given some gift, even if it is only a token, so that each will come to experience the pleasure of others as an occasion for personal satisfaction.

The view according to which attitudes of benevolence follow from group identification is as plausible as the one just discussed. To identify with others is by definition to break down psychological barriers: to incorporate others into one's own experience or what comes to the same thing, to extend the boundaries of one's own experience so as to include others. It follows automatically, therefore, that to the extent that we do actually identify with others their joys and sorrows become our joys and sorrows, their welfare becomes important to us personally because in an important sense their welfare is our own. Thus, in this view society encourages benevolence by providing social settings that favor the development of strong group ties. For example, children should not be educated at home alone under the supervision of parents or tutors but in classrooms with other children. And within the classroom children should not be pitted against one another in competitive contests but assigned group projects and given group rewards.

Cooperativeness and Competitiveness

As already noted, in calling humankind a social animal one of the things meant is gregariousness, or the inborn tendency of human beings to seek out one another's company. A second, and even more important, aspect of human sociality is human interdependence. Certain animal species live a solitary existence with the exception of brief periods for mating and nurturing the young. Humankind, however, could not even survive, much less prosper materially, if its members did not form stable and permanent communities. Even most noneconomic human activities are joint ventures. Theatrical productions, opera, symphony orchestras, team sports, political campaigning, and so forth are all group efforts. Successful human living, therefore, requires a great measure of *cooperativeness*, which we define as a set of dispositions to appreciate human values and goals that can be achieved only through group effort and to work effectively with others to realize those values and goals.

Unfortunately, the extent of human interdependence is often obscured, especially in America, by the so-called "pioneer" tradition of individual self-sufficiency, a tradition often associated with Thomas Jefferson and Henry David Thoreau. In his famous book *Walden* Thoreau describes how as a mature adult he managed to build a small cabin in the country and achieve an unusual degree of economic self-sufficiency. It is too easily forgotten that the possibility of Thoreau's experiment in self-sufficiency was itself a result of the painful collective experience of humankind. Like the fictitious Robinson Crusoe, Thoreau was able to survive physically in relative isolation only because in earlier life he fell heir to a sum of knowledge that the human species had accumulated slowly and with great difficulty. A child who ventured forth into the wilderness before acquiring this knowledge would have almost no chance of survival. Like the primitive tribesperson, this child would have to settle for whatever shelter could be found in caves or underbrush and would have to eat raw whatever could be hunted or gathered with two hands. But unlike primitive tribespersons, who shared the results of their economic efforts with other members of the community, the isolated child would have no insurance against a succession of bad days.

Moreover, even the mature adult with the benefit of humankind's collective historical experience is practically helpless alone in the face of earthquakes, hurricanes, failing health, disease, and other misfortunes. Thoreau's experiment, it should be remembered, lasted only a few years. Jefferson was, therefore, more realistic when he took as his ideal the material self-sufficiency of the family rather than of the isolated individual and when he simultaneously applauded the pioneer ideal of friendly and cooperative neighborliness. Contrary to popular belief most pioneer homes were not built by single individuals or even by single families. Most were built by groups of families who acted as informal mutual aid societies.

Thus, humankind is a social animal in the sense that even basic physical survival requires a high degree of cooperativeness. And, of course, the size of the primary economic unit and the degree of interdependence increase enormously when to the goal of mere physical survival is added the kind of material well-being made possible by modern technology and advances in medical knowledge. In today's world, for good or ill, the factory has replaced the individual artisan, and research teams have replaced the solitary inventor like Thomas Edison. Without a high degree of cooperativeness neither the individual nor the species could survive. But for cooperativeness we would immediately fall into a Hobbesian state of nature in which each is warring against all and life is "solitary, poor, nasty, brutish, and short."

Nothing said thus far means, however, that in modern life there is no place for *competitiveness,* which we define as the disposition to distinguish oneself by outperforming others. First, there are still relatively solitary occupations and activities in which competition on a person-to-person basis is socially valuable or at least socially acceptable. For example, writers, Olympic skiers, and concert violinists tend to compete on a person-to-person basis with socially desirable results. Second, there is plenty of room for healthy competition at the group level, both within the group and among rival groups. A fullback's desire to excel personally ordinarily benefits the team, and collective rivalry with other teams is often an important part of team spirit.

Humankind's extreme social interdependence does, however, have two implications for competitive activities. First, competitive rivalry must not be encouraged, or tolerated, except for socially useful or acceptable goals. For example, if Adam Smith is right in thinking that the primary effect of unrestrained competition for private profit is an abundance of low-priced, quality goods, then business competition should be encouraged. If, on the other hand, the principal effect of business competition for private profit is, as the Marxists argue, the division of society into an exploiting class and an exploited class, then competition for profit must be discouraged.

The second, closely related point is that in order to secure a proper measure of social stability and social harmony competition must normally take place within a context of socially devised rules that show a proper respect for justice. As we saw earlier, justice does not require strict equality, or even strict equality of opportunity. Social utility clearly requires that those with a natural athletic build have an advantage in the competitive struggle for distinction in sports, that those with exceptional intelligence have an advantage in the competitive struggle for distinction in the intellectual community, and so forth. But unless social utility dictates otherwise, justice does require that the rules of competitive struggle show a regard for the needs and deserts of the interested parties. When, for example, in the competitive struggle for wealth and privilege, rewards result more from luck or accident such as being well-born than from effort and sacrifice, it is almost inevitable that grave social tensions will build up. And the same thing is true when a society disregards the victims of "natural" injustices (for example, the intellectually and physically handicapped) or the victims of social injustices (for example, those who because they have been born in poor neighborhoods receive inferior education). Unless carefully controlled, every competitive contest carries within it the seeds of social decay and threatens to produce a lawless and unscrupulous Hobbesian war of each against all.

There are also certain facts about competitive struggle that everyone should consider not simply out of social concern but out of regard for one's own psychological well-being. First, anyone tempted by a prize to be won through competitive contest should remember that competitive contests often have a momentum of their own. There is normally no natural limit, no cut-off point. For example, the person who squeezes out colleagues in competition for a job at a higher rung of the corporate ladder does not ordinarily stand still once the initial objective is achieved. Instead, the person once launched in this direction tends to engage in another contest for still another competitive prize. Competitive struggle, therefore, is unlikely to be very satisfying unless one likes the struggle itself. Second, because of the momentum of competitive struggle and because normally the higher one aspires the tougher the competition, competitors often find themselves sorely frustrated and strongly tempted to bend or break the rules. It is a fact of life that as the prize becomes greater the competition tends to become not only more intense but more unscrupulous. And it is probably the nature of competitive struggle—rather than power itself, as popularly supposed—that accounts for so much corruption in high offices. Finally, whether competitors play by the rules or not, if they are successful they are likely to have many enemies. It is for this reason that the mighty so often fall, to the scarcely concealed delight of their "inferiors."

Idealism

As we shall be using the term, an *idealistic person* is someone who is disposed to make a serious effort or sacrifice to effect desired social changes. The sacrifices idealists make are normally motivated by benevolence and conscientiousness, their ambition being to help create a society with less suffering and less injustice. But benevolence and conscientiousness by themselves are not enough, since no matter how disturbed one may be by the spectacle of human suffering and social injustice, one is unlikely to act on behalf of social reform if one believes that whatever one might do would be fruitless or counterproductive. In other words, to understand idealists we must normally assume that they believe in the possibility of effecting social change through personal sacrifice or effort.

Depending on the degree of personal sacrifice they are prepared to make idealists fall into a fairly wide spectrum, ranging from someone like Che Guevara, who many times over risked his life, to mild liberal democrats who are prepared to give some time and money but will not risk their person or social status. Depending on the means they think proper to bring about social change idealists also fall into a fairly wide spectrum. To make this discussion more manageable, however, we shall use a two-fold classification. First, there are those who believe that significant social progress can be achieved peacefully through legal means provided that the form of government is democratic. Second, there are those who believe that significant social progress can be achieved only by violent or illegal actions even within a society that is formally democratic.

The position of the first group is relatively simple, and if one accepts the premise that it is possible to achieve substantial change peacefully through democratic institutions it is not very controversial. Members of this group urge us to vote, to become party workers, to run for political office. They urge us to publicize and protest against social wrongs by all legal means: letters to editors, street pamphleteering, participation in political marches and demonstrations, lobbying, striking, and so on. And, of course, they urge us to back any public policies that will help to produce a more rational, more benevolent, and more conscientious electorate.

The problematic position philosophically is that of the more militant idealists who are prepared to use violence or illegal acts. There is no way of denying the basic human need for stability or the importance of a widely observed legal system as a means of maintaining it. Nor is it possible to deny that violence does injury to persons or to property. This is a part of the meaning of "violence." It follows that illegal or violent activities must always be morally suspect. It does not, however, follow that violent or illegal acts are never justified. Almost everyone believes that violent and illegal means are justified to fight tyranny. There is, however, always a presumption against violent or illegal acts, and persons who recommend or perform them must be able to present a good case in their own defense.

What, then, are the kinds of conditions that must normally exist to justify violent or illegal acts?

The "Failure" of Democracy. First, there must be good reason to believe that peaceful and legal means for correcting social evils are either nonexistent or intolerably slow. If a society is formally democratic, this means showing that its democratic institutions do not function properly. We touched briefly on this problem in the last chapter and will make a few additional comments here.

Consider this problem as it presents itself in connection with one alleged social evil—namely, the unjust distribution of wealth represented by huge private fortunes. Most militant idealists, contrary to popular belief, do not urge strict equality in the distribution of material goods. Rather, they accept inequalities provided that they correspond to the criteria of justice such as need, merit, and social utility. But, they say, in capitalist countries inequalities do not correspond even roughly to the criteria of justice, and throughout the long history of capitalist democracies every legal and nonviolent effort to correct unjust equalities has failed. Of the many multi-million dollar fortunes in the United States, they argue, most have been acquired through inheritance or marriage rather than through work. And of those that have been acquired through work, the vast majority have not been acquired by socially useful services but by socially useless or socially pernicious acts. The old saying that behind every great fortune there lies a crime is only a slight exaggeration. These "facts" about the great fortunes have been widely recognized for well over a century, and throughout that period the majority of the people has enthusiastically favored remedial measures. But from the days of the "robber barons" in the middle of the nineteenth century until the present the will of the majority has been effectively negated. Still today most of the robber baron families hold their fortunes intact. Tax loopholes and other measures favoring the very rich are a staple feature of democratic capitalist societies.

In response to these arguments several points are usually made. First, it is argued that citizens should have the right to dispose of their wealth as they see fit. Most especially, it is said, the right to share one's wealth with one's spouse and one's children has a value of its own and must be preserved even at the cost of some inequities in the distribution of wealth. Second, although wealth is frequently acquired in capitalist societies through shady deals, the so-called "robber barons" and other captains of industry also perform inestimable social services as entrepreneurs. Without large rewards for people of great ambition, shrewdness, and managerial skill material progress would be seriously slowed down. Finally, it is fortunate that the elected representatives of the majority have the good sense to defeat the will of the masses where great fortunes are concerned. For the desire of the masses to destroy these fortunes reflects not a considered judgment concerning social justice but merely the resentment of the mediocre and the unsuccessful.

The Magnitude of the Evils to Be Corrected. Second, violent or illegal acts cannot be justified unless there is good reason to believe that the evils to be corrected are severe or widespread. It is almost unnecessary to say that good judgment in these matters is a difficult achievement. There are, however, two important considerations that must constantly be borne in mind if our judgment is not to go astray. First, there is a strong tendency based on simple self-interest and wishful thinking for those who are personally well-off within any given society to blind themselves to the magnitude of its evils, and a corresponding tendency for those who have personally suffered from a society's evils to magnify those evils. Second, partly because most societies foster social cohesion with exaggerated claims of national superiority and partly because the privileged within any society normally have the greatest power to shape public opinion, most people —unless self-interest is directly involved—have a decided tendency to underestimate the social evils of their society. For both of these reasons no society can hope for disinterested or impartial judgments in these delicate matters unless it is seriously committed to fostering rationality.

The Legacy of Violence. Finally, violent or illegal acts cannot be justified unless there is reason to believe that these acts will actually further the ends for which they were designed and will not create evils comparable to or greater than those they are intended to abolish or mitigate. On matters like these good judgment is again a difficult achievement. But here, too, it will help if certain considerations are given their proper weight.

First, violent or illegal action very often leaves a legacy of bitterness that endangers achievement of the goals sought. Blind moral indignation and unfocused rage are more often than not counterproductive, leading to what many leftist political groups condemn as "political adventurism."

Second, the qualities that tend to make revolutionary leaders successful—for example, ruthlessness, single-minded dedication, belligerence, impatience, suspiciousness—are often enormous handicaps in the process of reconstruction that follows successful revolution. Yet, few revolutionaries step down once they have acquired power. Thus, as in the case of Stalin, a valued leader in pre-revolutionary days becomes an odious tyrant in the post-revolutionary period. Speaking more generally, the habits of lawlessness and violence acquired in the idealistic quest for greater justice are not easily shed and may very well persist beyond the set of circumstances that is initially thought to justify them.

Self-Discipline

By a *self-disciplined* person we mean someone (a) who is disposed to postpone immediate gratification or to make other sacrifices for the sake of distant goals and (b) who tends to establish goals and assign priorities through planning, reflection, or deliberation. It should be noted, however, that self-disciplined people do not stop to reflect every time they are called on to act. Often, especially in familiar situations that fall into established patterns, they rely on long-standing habits. But to the extent that these persons are well-disciplined, their habits were initially formed after rational deliberation and therefore represent a second, civilized nature as opposed to a first, instinctive nature that owes nothing to rationality. By an undisciplined person, on the other hand, we mean someone with little capacity for pursuing distant goals, a tendency to act impulsively or capriciously rather than deliberately or reflectively, and a poorly developed second, civilized nature.

In all societies highly self-disciplined individuals are rare. And where self-discipline does exist it is not likely to be a generalized personality trait. For example, someone who is remarkably self-disciplined in some specialized area of athletics is often totally undisciplined outside that area. Moreover, a number of social critics have said that self-discipline, even in specialized areas, is becoming rarer and rarer in contemporary capitalist societies.

Several reasons for the alleged decline in self-discipline have been offered. Some social critics trace it to the demise of laissez-faire capitalism and the steady increase in measures designed to promote social welfare. Self-discipline, they say, is a trait of the rugged individualist and the capitalist entrepreneur, not of the person who looks to the government to supply every need.

Others attribute the alleged decline in self-discipline less to the growing role of government than to the inner dynamics of the capitalist system itself. In its early stages, they say, capitalism must force people to save in order to accumulate investment capital. But in its later stages capitalism must force people to spend, since in these later stages consumer spending rather than savings becomes the principal motor of economic progress. Thus, advanced capitalism fosters the so-called "consumer society" through such devices as heavy advertising, attractive packaging, and installment buying. The popular mentality becomes one of impulse buying and "Buy now, pay later."

It has also been said that because of aversion to public spending and a heavy reliance on the private profit motive capitalist societies have become increasingly passive, spectator societies rather than societies of doers. Professional and televised sports, for example, are big businesses from which great profits are made. But involving large numbers of people in sports as players would require huge public expenditures for free or low-cost recreation centers that only socialist countries seem willing to make.

Finally, there are those who say that self-discipline is disappearing because of the growing interdependence of human beings due to advanced technology. In a socially interdependent world planning must be made collectively rather than individually. Private individuals must fit in as best they can. There are simply fewer areas of life in which individual planning is possible.

Nonetheless, no matter how reduced the space for private planning may be and no matter what social pressures may impede its practice, both the individual and society would benefit from greater self-discipline. Rest and relaxation have their proper place in life. And there are a few cases of overdisciplined people—people who so exclusively concentrate on the distant future that they neglect the here and now or people whose planning is so rigid and detailed that they practically invite failure through inflexibility. But most of us err most of the time on the side of too little rather than too much self-discipline. It would, for example, be difficult to say what percentage of the American population has chosen a career or vocation after a careful assessment of individual strengths and weaknesses and after a diligent attempt to establish the objective range of available options. But, surely, many individual tragedies and much social waste could have been prevented if more people had done so. Similarly, it is difficult to say how many people have used their intelligence and their imagination in an attempt to foresee what life would be like after a contemplated marriage. But, surely, many lives have been blighted because couples just drifted into marriage without a proper regard for their own future welfare, much less that of future offspring.

Unfortunately, individuals who are insufficiently disciplined often take comfort and inspiration in ideas that have filtered down through the philosophical tradition. As we saw in Chapter One, many people justify a disregard for ordinary prudence in terms of a conception of time that accords greater reality to the present than it does to the past, which provides the basis for planning, and to the future, for the sake of which planning is normally undertaken.

There are also those who have been influenced by excessively individualistic theories of selfhood to overlook the pervasiveness of human sociality and to assume that civilized traits acquired through socialization and discipline are merely a superficial mask. Behind this mask, they say, lies the true self. And in the name of "sincerity," "spontaneity," or "naturalness," they justify every imaginable vice and weakness. The fact is, however, that socially acquired and disciplined habits or dispositions are at least as deep and profound parts of the human person as instincts and native temperamental peculiarities. The latter are hardly more than the raw materials out of which the individual self is forged. Almost all truly admirable instances of naturalness and spontaneity are expressions of an individual's second, civilized nature. For example, the unforced, flowing grace of accomplished gymnasts is essentially a product of discipline. One need only compare gymnasts' movements after training with their first feeble and awkward efforts. There is, therefore, no contradiction between discipline and spontaneity. The contradiction is rather between discipline and caprice or whim. And it is simply perverse to think that we can betray ourselves by living up to the best in our nature. Our raw, undisciplined, unsocialized impulses have no automatic right to expression and no special privilege to speak in our name.

Chapter 5

Religion and Morality

In the popular mind religion and morality are often closely related. It is said that in a world beset with suffering and evil only a religious orientation offers a genuine chance for personal well-being. At the same time it is said that a decline of religion would substantially diminish respect for moral rules. These views have relatively few supporters among moral philosophers today. Many philosophers feel that religion does make a positive contribution both to personal well-being and to right conduct, but most attribute at least equal importance to nonreligious factors. And some philosophers have been very critical of religion, arguing that it actually reduces chances for personal happiness, undermines moral conduct, and impedes social progress. In this chapter we shall discuss the basic issues in this controversy.

First, however, a general word of caution is in order. Each of the world's major religions differs in important respects from the others. Even within a single religion, such as Christianity, there are important differences among its adherents. Few, if any, of the points raised in this chapter, therefore, apply to all religious orientations.

Religion and the "Meaning of Life"

Religion, it is said, contributes to personal well-being by giving life "meaning." Without religion we are lost and at sea. This claim is supported in four principal ways.

The Need for a Nonrational World View. Religion is supposed to satisfy a deeply rooted human need to believe by providing answers to questions that reason or science has not yet been able to answer and perhaps never will. Of course, some religions do not make this particular claim, since they believe that their religious world view is rationally defensible. But most religious believers readily grant that their world view rests largely on faith, not reason.

Despite the spectacular achievements of modern science almost no one disputes that the current scientific world picture is sketchy. Science does not answer all of our questions.

Nearly everyone also grants that most human beings have a limited tolerance for uncertainty and rational discipline. Rationality demands, among other things, that we subject our socially inherited beliefs to critical examination and that we reserve judgment when evidence is unavailable. But these practices have never been popular. Socrates was put to death for having insisted too much upon them. And in almost all contemporary societies the person who openly adheres to these practices runs serious risks. Most people want so badly to believe they have answers to the important questions that they tend to accept uncritically the first answers that come along. And this spontaneous psychological disposition is usually reinforced by parental and other social pressures. It is not, therefore, surprising that most people born in Christian societies profess Christianity; most people born in Hindu societies, Hinduism; most people born in Islamic cultures, Islam; and so forth.

Many people seem to believe that the near universality of the tendency to profess a world view for which no rational warrant exists is sufficient evidence for the desirability of a nonrational world view. But this inference is not legitimate. The most that the widespread tendency to adopt a nonrational world view could prove is that such a world view provides a measure of immediate psychological comfort. It does not prove that nonrational world views are in the best all-round, long-range interests of those who adopt them. The tendency of human beings to prefer immediate gratification to long-term well-being is beyond dispute. And this tendency is as strong in matters of belief as in anything else. Moreover, it is easy to establish the existence of many near universal beliefs—for example, belief in the inferiority of outgroups—whose overall undesirability is clear.

As already indicated, the principal objection to the adoption of a nonrational world view is that it violates standards of rationality.

Later in this chapter we will say more in this regard. Here we wish to consider only one aspect of this objection: namely, that given the conditions of modern life, a nonrational world view is difficult to sustain and can therefore bring little psychological comfort to the individual.

One of the major features of modern life that supposedly reduces the vitality of nonrational world views is its open, pluralistic character. The reasoning is as follows: It appears to be difficult, perhaps impossible, for us to believe something is true when we know there is no rational basis for believing it. It is, for example, difficult to believe by a simple act of will that it is going to rain tomorrow. In the absence of any rational basis for this belief, such as a weather report by a competent meteorologist, the desire to believe it is going to rain simply does not produce conviction. So it is with religious belief. Societies have been able to indoctrinate the young in religious belief only by persuading them that there is a rational basis for that belief. Typically, the child accepts religious teachings on the authority of parents or society in the way that adults accept weather reports by competent meteorologists. The child does not know what the evidence for religious belief is, but the child does believe that evidence exists. And in a closed, homogeneous society, where a single religious world view prevails and no challenge to that world view is permitted, this childhood indoctrination may well last a lifetime. In the open, pluralistic societies most of us live in today, however, the child inevitably learns that there are many different religious authorities and that it is harder for these authorities to establish their credentials than it is for meteorologists to establish theirs. In the process of discovering this, the child's religious belief is seriously undermined. The emotional attachment to the religion in which one was reared may well persist, but firm conviction or robust belief in its doctrines fades. Moreover, for those who have been taught that religious doubt is sinful or a sign of divine disfavor religious doubt can result in considerable distress.

In addition to the growing pluralism of modern society, which pits one religious authority against another, there are a number of historical developments that tend to undermine all uncritical reliance on authority. The individual is, therefore, forced to question not only the superiority of one nonrational world view over others but also the acceptability of any nonrational religious outlook at all. Just as modern times have forced us to abandon tribal rain dances and religious prayers in favor of scientific agricultural methods, so modern times are credited with forcing us to abandon religious world views in favor of a scientific world view. The rapidly accelerating rate of historical change, the increasingly complex technology, the growing commitment to individual freedom—each of these developments makes authority a less reliable guide and obliges us to adopt a more critical and scientific mentality. Of course, some people do succeed more or less in compartmentalizing their minds, adopting one method for the formation of religious belief and another for the formation of belief in practical affairs. But there appear to be definite limits to compartmentalization. A rational mental set is not easily turned on and off. Those who exercise due scientific caution in one area of belief cannot easily allow prejudice to dominate in another. And those who do are likely to suffer from what psychologists sometimes call "cognitive dissonance," an uncomfortable sense of being at odds with oneself.

A Cosmic Role for Humankind. It is said that religious orientations not only satisfy the need for a world view but also the need to believe that human beings have an honorable and dignified place in the world. This claim has not played an important role in the Eastern religions but it has played an important role in Judaism, Christianity, and Islam. It also underlies much of the science–versus–religion controversy of the contemporary Western world.

Since the beginning of modern science in the sixteenth century the Biblical world view of the Jewish, Christian, and Islamic traditions has met two great challenges. First, Copernicus and others overthrew the traditional view that the earth is the center of the universe. The current scientific view is that the earth is an insignificant speck in the cosmos, merely one relatively small planet in one relatively small solar system in one relatively small galaxy. Second, in the nineteenth century Darwin and others undermined the traditional view that humankind is a special creation of God and that the rest of creation was made for our benefit. The current scientific view is that humankind is a product of a long evolutionary process and that like other animal species, who are products of similar evolutionary processes, human beings may eventually be displaced by new animal species better equipped to survive. Thus, we are confronted by a choice between a nonscientific religious world view according to which humankind is at the center of a universe created for our benefit by God and a scientific world view according to which human history is a minor unfinished episode taking place in a tiny corner of the universe and without the slightest cosmic significance. The religious view, it is said, gives us a sense of dignity or worth; the scientific view belittles and demoralizes us.

It is arguable, however, whether the individual human being's sense of personal worth is in fact as closely related to a conception of the role of the human species within the cosmos as religionists seem to assume. Human beings tend to identify not with humankind as a whole but with specific human communities.

It is also arguable whether the individual's sense of worth *should* depend to any serious extent upon an identification with the species. We do not find it wholesome or wise for members of a small nation with a relatively unglorious history to allow themselves to suffer in self-esteem because of their country's insignificance on the international scene. Why, then, should we allow ourselves to suffer in self-esteem because the human species is cosmically insignificant? Neither do we find it wise or wholesome for members of a large nation with a glorious national tradition to take personal credit for that tradition. And why should the chauvinism of the species be any more defensible, especially if humankind's privileged status in the cosmos is due not to human efforts but to divine bounty? Actually, the scientific conception of humankind's status in the world, from which it follows that human achievements must be attributed to human striving in the face of an indifferent cosmos, provides a far more legitimate basis for human pride than the religious perspective according to which our status is determined by God.

Divine Love. The third argument for the view that religion gives meaning to life is based on the contention that the religious world view affords human beings consolation in times of distress. For according to many religious orientations human beings are not simply the central characters in the created order, they are also the children of a loving God. The presence of God as loving father, as someone who cares for the individual as a father cares for his children and to whom the individual may turn in prayer, is a source of warmth and comfort.

Critics of this claim ordinarily make several points. First, it is said that the religious conception of God has always been complex and contradictory. On the one hand, God is represented as loving, merciful, and indulgent. On the other hand, he is represented as wrathful, stern, and uncompromising. More often than not, therefore, the conception of a stern God cancels out the conception of a merciful God.

Second, it is argued that if an individual does have a conception of God in which love and mercy predominate, this is so not because of religious teaching but because of childhood experience. The individual's image of God tends regularly to reflect childhood experience. If the earthly father is loving, then so is the divine father. If the earthly father is stern, so is the divine father. In other words, religionists put the cart before the horse. It is not the concept of a loving God that gives a sense of being at home in the universe. It is a sense of being at home in the universe that gives a concept of a loving God.

Finally, it is said that the adult who turns to God for consolation in times of distress is courting disappointment. A mature adult in times of distress seeks psychological support from other human beings. It is true, of course, that support from other human beings is not always forthcoming. But, according to religion's critics, support from a fantasized father substitute is even less reliable. Moreover, the habit of seeking support from God is not conducive to building the kinds of solid human relationships from which reliable support can reasonably be expected.

Immortality. Finally, there is the argument according to which religion gives meaning to life by encouraging the hope of a continued existence beyond the grave, an afterlife so radiantly happy that we will be compensated for all the misery and suffering we have experienced in our earthly life. Without religion, it is added, there is no satisfactory way of coping with the fact of death.

The desirability of an afterlife is so much taken for granted today that it often comes as something of a surprise to learn that in the fourth century B.C. Epicurus thought that he was rendering human beings a great service by demonstrating the impossibility of personal immortality. The fact is, however, that in Epicurus' day the afterlife was regarded as a humiliating, shadowy existence to be shunned by any rational person. The afterlife was portrayed in even gloomier terms throughout the greater part of Christian history. Until recently the orthodox Christian view was that the vast majority of human beings would suffer eternally in hell after the Last Judgment. The blissful afterlife was reserved exclusively for a small number of the elect. It is only recently that hope for an eternal reward has come to predominate over the fear of fire and brimstone.

For our purposes here, however, we shall confine our attention to the view that human beings not only live on after physical death but live on in bliss. Our question is whether such a view contributes to our well-being in the here and now. Most persons who answer this question negatively grant that the person who is fully and firmly persuaded of a happy afterlife may be spared much anguish. They also ordinarily grant that in a society where the belief in a blissful afterlife is carefully inculcated in the young and where challenges to that belief are strictly forbidden, the dogma of immortality might command unwavering adherence. But once again nonreligionists tend to argue that in today's world it is a most unusual individual whose belief in personal survival after death is strong and unshakable. According to a saying that circulated during World War II, there are no atheists in foxholes. The human need to believe in an afterlife is so strong that it crushes all doubts as death approaches. Many nonreligionists argue, however, that the opposite is true. No matter how strong, the will to believe cannot survive a confrontation with the reality of physical death. It is precisely in foxholes that religion is tried and found wanting, that believers become atheists.

Moreover, it has been plausibly maintained by the seventeenth-century Jewish philosopher Baruch Spinoza, among others, that nothing encourages the fear of physical death more than the effort to believe in personal survival after physical death. According to Spinoza, fear feeds on hope, and as long as religious leaders dangle the hope of an afterlife before our eyes we shall be infected by the fear of death. The best and only rational way to cope with the fear of death is to immerse ourselves in life. In Spinoza's words: "A free man thinks of nothing less than of death, and his wisdom is not a meditation upon death but upon life."

In sum, the most common traditional technique for dealing with the fear of death—namely, denying death and affirming personal immortality—is said to be ineffective not only because reason fails to support the hope for personal immortality but also because efforts to believe in the absence of evidence simply produce an unhealthy preoccupation with death. A much more promising technique is a wholesome commitment to this-worldly pursuits.

Mystical Experience

Religion is alleged to contribute to the good life not only by giving life meaning but also by providing short-lived though extremely intense experiences of a mystical nature. These experiences seem to occur in all parts of the world and in all cultures. And there is reason to believe that they are even more widespread than is often supposed, since many people who have had them keep the fact to themselves either through fear of ridicule or because of an inability to describe what they have experienced.

From descriptions by the more articulate mystics it appears that these experiences—despite important differences in interpretation—have a common experiential core. Three principal features may be distinguished. First, the world of ordinary everyday experience and the ordinary everyday self lose their prominence in consciousness and are seen as superficial or insignificant. Second, contact appears to be made with a deeper and more profound reality that underlies the everyday world and the everyday self. This underlying reality appears to have a unity and cohesiveness that contrasts sharply with the diversity, plurality, and conflicting goals of everyday experience. Finally, there is a sense that the everyday world and everyday self are fading away and being absorbed in the deeper, underlying reality, where all is one.

Reports on the emotional quality of the mystical state all stress its exceptional intensity. Although short-lived and infrequent, the experiences are extremely vivid. In addition, most reports describe the experience as highly positive. Terms like "pleasurable" or "agreeable" are inadequate. Terms like "sublime," "ecstatic," and "rapturous" are closer to the mark. Significantly, however, the experience is almost never wholly positive. Nearly all the religious mystics report that the feelings of sublimity are mixed with feelings of dread, fear, awe, or "holy terror."

Little is known about the causes of mystic experience. Many of the world's famous mystics believed that the experience was associated with certain ascetic, or self-denying, practices such as sexual abstinence, fasting, and even various forms of self-punishment. The experience has also been associated with various forms of prayer and meditation. Among many mystics, especially in the Far East, breathing exercises and certain forms of physical relaxation accompany the use of prayer or meditation. Some American Indian tribes use drugs to induce the experience. Most mystical experiences, however, are probably not associated with any of the practices just mentioned, occurring spontaneously without preparation or advance notice of any kind. And despite a common misconception to the contrary the experience is clearly not limited to those who are religiously oriented. Jean-Paul Sartre, whose orientation is atheist and wholly secular, has given unmistakable accounts of the experience that are clearly based on personal experience.

Whatever triggers the experience, most mystics value it not only as an intrinsic good of an exceptionally high order but also as a valid insight into the nature of reality. Often, they see in it proof that there is in fact a greater reality than that to which we have access through our physical senses in the ordinary conduct of life and that it is possible to obliterate the ego and to unite with that greater reality.

There is, however, a nonreligious interpretation of the experience that not only casts doubt on its validity as a source of knowledge but also calls into question the enormous intrinsic value normally claimed for it. According to this interpretation the everyday world of normal waking adult consciousness and the mature self with its desires and mental sets have been slowly shaped over a long and difficult period of socialization and individual self-discipline. They are the end products of a process begun in infancy or possibly in the fetus when the concepts of self and world, or even inner and outer, were unformed. At that time the physical senses were so poorly developed and undiscriminating that the outside world was hardly more than a blob. And the consciousness of self was meager or nonexistent. Accordingly, the mystical experience, in which the everyday world and the mature self dissolve into an undifferentiated unity, is nothing but a regression to the primitive fetal or infantile stage of life. The intensely pleasurable quality of the experience is attributed to the relaxation of the tensions and discipline of civilized social existence. The nameless dread or fear that usually accompanies this pleasure is said to represent the acute sense of loss that any adult must experience when cut off from the common social world and the civilized self that interacts with this world. And the brevity of the mystical experience is explained by assuming that the weight of past experience quickly forces us back into the mold of the everyday world and the everyday self.

Thus, an experience that religionists have traditionally construed as rapturous union with God is interpreted by many nonbelievers today as a momentary disorientation in which the individual simultaneously experiences a highly pleasurable release from the usual constraints of social living and a painful sense of separation from everything that gives weight and substance to life. If traditional religionists emphasized the positive aspect of the experience and understated the negative aspect, the nonbeliever would probably say that they did so because they found it difficult to reconcile this negative aspect with their interpretation of the experience as a union with God. Sartre, who had no religious preconceptions, emphasized the negative aspects of the experience and actually referred to it as the experience of "nausea."

It should be noted, however, that Sartre agrees with the religious mystics in ascribing to the mystical experience significance as a source of knowledge. What, he asks, but popular prejudice could lead one to believe that the real world would be presented to us in everyday sense-experience?

The Moral Code and Divine Commands

A famous line from one of the novels of Dostoevsky says: "If God does not exist, everything is permitted." This line is susceptible to two interpretations. According to one interpretation morally right and morally wrong acts are by definition acts commanded or forbidden by God. If, therefore, God does not exist, there is no such thing as right or wrong behavior and we may do whatever we wish. According to a second interpretation, human beings are motivated to perform right acts and to refrain from wrong acts by religious beliefs, such as the belief in heavenly rewards and punishments in hell. If, therefore, there is no God, once again we are free to do whatever we wish, because we have no incentive to observe the moral code. In this section we shall examine the first of these views.

General questions relating to right and wrong conduct will be discussed in Chapter Six. Here we shall be concerned exclusively with what is sometimes called the *theological principle,* according to which in the last analysis an act is wrong because God forbids it and right because God wills it. Stated in slightly different terms, the theological principle holds that any acceptable definition of right and wrong behavior has to be couched in terms of the divine will.

Before continuing, it should be made clear that those who reject the theological principle do not necessarily reject either the existence or the moral goodness of God. It is quite possible to believe both that God exists and that he wills right behavior while not believing that right behavior is right because God wills it—or, what comes to the same thing, without believing that a right act is by definition an act willed by God. An analogy might make this point clearer. All of us do in fact believe that human beings exist and that human beings are less than ten feet tall. Yet none of us believes that human beings are human because they are under ten feet tall or that being human is by definition a matter of being under ten feet tall.

In one of Plato's most interesting dialogues, the *Euthyphro,* Plato had Socrates challenge someone who held to the theological principle by asking him whether the view that an act is right because God wills it is compatible with the view that God wills an act because it is right. In elaborating on the meaning of this challenge Socrates presented an argument according to which the theological principle involves us in a vicious logical circle. Stated loosely, Socrates' argument goes as follows: God is by definition a morally good being. The proof of this is that we would refuse to call any being "God" unless he were morally good, just as we would refuse to call any figure a triangle unless it had exactly three sides. It follows that in order to know whether any being alleged to be God is really God we must first know whether that being is morally good, just as in order to know whether any geometrical figure is a triangle we must first determine whether it has exactly three sides. If, however, moral goodness is defined in terms of God's will—or, if an act is right simply because God wills it—then we have to know that God exists and what he wills before we can know what is morally good. Thus, if we grant that God is by definition morally good while simultaneously holding that God's will defines moral goodness, we find ourselves in the following situation: We cannot determine whether God exists until we have determined antecedently and independently what moral goodness is. But we cannot determine what moral goodness is antecedently and independently because by definition moral goodness is what God wills.

The point of Socrates' argument can be stated less abstractly in terms of alleged divine revelations. And little is lost by restating the argument in these terms, since few people claim direct acquaintance with God. Most persons claim to know God only through his revelations. Suppose, then, that a form suddenly appears before us, stating that it is an emissary from God. Suppose, further, that this form declares that Moses was a false prophet whose ten commandments were dictated by the Devil. The form then announces the true commandments—among them, commit a murder a day, tell ten lies a day, torture your enemies, and break all promises. Needless to say, we would reject the form's claim to reveal God's will. And we would do so because we are persuaded that God is good and that what the form commands is evil. But—and this is the crucial point—if an act is right because God wills it, we are not justified in rejecting an alleged revelation from God simply because we think what it commands is evil. If

God wills murdering, lying, and torturing, then murdering, lying, and torturing are right. The fact that we do appeal to the moral content of alleged revelations in order to determine their authenticity shows that our concept of right and wrong is logically prior to and independent of our concept of God. It is, therefore, a mistake to think that we must get our ideas of right and wrong from God. It is in the light of our ideas of right and wrong that we frame our idea of God.

Religious Sanctions

As we just saw, the claim that God's nonexistence is disastrous to morality may mean that in the absence of God there can be no legitimate moral code. As we also saw, however, it may mean that in the absence of God there is no incentive for obeying the moral code. Many people who hold one of these beliefs also hold the other. Nonetheless, the two beliefs are independent. And there are more and more religionists who believe that right and wrong are issues that must be decided on a nonreligious basis but who at the same time believe that religion provides motives for right action. In other words, increasingly religionists are rejecting the view that religion tells us what we ought to do while holding fast to the view that religion inspires us to live up to our moral ideals. It is this latter belief that will concern us here.

Among those who see religion as a source of moral energy, or an incentive to right conduct, a further distinction must be made. Some believe that religion is absolutely essential to right conduct, while others believe that religion simply reinforces or supplements nonreligious incentives. The view that religious incentives are absolutely essential was once widely held. The seventeenth-century English philosopher John Locke argued that atheists ought not to be allowed to testify in court, since their atheism made them wholly unreliable witnesses. Even many eighteenth-century Enlightenment figures such as Voltaire and Benjamin Franklin held that only the fear of hell kept most people in line. This was the meaning of Voltaire's famous remark that if God did not exist he would have to be invented. Most religionists today, however, take a more moderate view and attach greater weight to nonreligious or purely social motivations. Religious motives for right conduct are seen as helpful but not absolutely essential. How, then, is religion supposed to motivate right conduct?

Rewards and Punishment After Death. First, the incentive most often stressed historically is the belief in rewards and punishments after death. If, it is said, one believes that right conduct is rewarded with eternal bliss and wrong conduct punished with eternal suffering, surely one will be more inclined toward right behavior and less inclined toward wrong behavior. In passing, it should perhaps be pointed out that in many branches of Christianity the connection between right conduct and one's fate after death is either absent or weak. For example, Calvinists argue that we are all such miserable sinners in the eyes of God that none deserves a heavenly reward. God's choice of the elect, therefore, is made without regard to moral conduct. Here, however, we shall confine ourselves to the view that one's fate after death is tied primarily to one's moral conduct while in life. And in order to simplify the discussion further we shall limit our consideration to the negative religious sanction of eternal punishment in hell. The principles outlined can be easily adapted for the purpose of evaluating the positive sanction of rewards in heaven.

In general the effectiveness of negative sanctions, or punishments, is related to three different factors. One is the *severity* of the punishment. For example, a thirty-year prison sentence is ordinarily more effective than a thirty-day sentence. The second factor is the *certainty* that the punishment will be administered. If a certain kind of crime is punished nine times out of ten, for instance, the deterrent effect is ordinarily greater than if it is punished only three times out of ten. The third factor is the *immediacy* of the punishment. Given the human propensity to ignore long-term considerations, a punishment administered immediately after the commission of an offense is more effective than one administered months or years later. Just as we tend irrationally to prefer immediate gratifications to distant gratifications, so we tend irrationally to be more effectively deterred by the prospect of an immediate punishment than by the prospect of a postponed punishment.

The first question we ask, then, is how does the negative religious sanction of eternal punishment in hell rank in terms of these three factors? Clearly, the negative religious sanction ranks high in terms of severity. What could be more horrible than eternal torment in hell! But the negative religious sanction does not rank high in terms of certainty. Even under circumstances that are most favorable to religious belief, it is doubtful that people will be as certain of punishment in hell as they are of negative social sanctions. Prisons, scaffolds, fines, social snubs, and the like are undeniable realities. The beliefs in God and hell are constantly challenged. Moreover, even those who are firmly persuaded that hell is the ultimate destination of the wicked must wonder from time to time whether their personal behavior could possibly be so evil as to merit eternal suffering. Moreover, if one believes that God is merciful as well as just, one would expect divine forgiveness. As far as immediacy is concerned, the religious sanction must also lag behind negative social sanctions, since by definition death is the last event in a person's life.

Second, how does severity rank as a deterrent when compared to certainty and immediacy? If severity were the major factor in determining the effectiveness of punishment, the negative religious sanction could be of great importance. But if certainty and immediacy are of relatively greater importance its effectiveness is considerably diminished. Unfortunately, there are no definitive studies of this question, and there is considerable room for controversy. It can be said, however, that among students of human behavior who have worked in this area there is a growing consensus that certainty and immediacy are in general substantially more effective as deterrents than severity. There is also a growing consensus of professional opinion that there is an irrational popular tendency to overestimate the importance of severity and to neglect or even overlook entirely the other two factors. The strength of the spontaneous human tendency to combat evil by increasing the severity rather than the certainty or immediacy of the penalties has led many thinkers to assume an inherently cruel streak in human nature. Whatever the cause, it does appear that the tendency in question, like wishful thinking, is one of those many irrational human dispositions that a civilized person must learn to counteract.

The All-knowing God. The second aspect of religion that comes up in discussions about its value as an incentive to right conduct is belief in the omniscience of God. Since human beings are fallible, or subject to error, it is possible for us to violate the established moral rules when it is in our interest to do so and to escape social punishments by concealing what we have done from society. Since, however, God is omniscient, or all-knowing, God cannot be so deceived. Accordingly, the believer in God will more consistently observe the established moral rules.

It seems that every society harbors a significant number of accomplished hypocrites who can give the appearance of observing the moral rules while secretly breaking them for their own benefit. And it is certainly true that all of us have at one time or another left ourselves open to the charge of moral hypocrisy. For this reason moral philosophers of all persuasions, religious and nonreligious, have almost unanimously insisted on the inadequacy of external social sanctions alone. If a society is to hold together the external sanctions must be supplemented by internal sanctions. There must be a generalized tendency toward benevolence, a tendency for people to be pleased by the well-being of others and pained by their suffering. And there must be some measure of conscientiousness, a tendency for people to suffer in self-esteem when they violate moral rules and to take personal pride in adhering to those rules. It is a commonplace in moral philosophy that internal sanctions such as these are not only indispensable but also superior to the external sanctions insofar as they are more certain and more immediate.

The question is thus whether, in addition to the internal sanctions of benevolence and conscientiousness, we wish to add an internal religious sanction in which adherence to moral rule is secured by a concept of God as an omniscient being who is watching our every move. And since an internal sanction of this character appears to be merely one variety of what Piaget called the immature conscience, or the internalization of parental or social commands obeyed out of fear, our attitude toward this internal sanction tends to duplicate our attitude toward the immature conscience. For many people, right behavior motivated by concern to stay in the good graces of an all-knowing God is merely a religious version of the Big Brother described in George Orwell's *1984*.

Religious Love. The third aspect of religion commonly seen as a motivation for right conduct is the religious emphasis on love. Sometimes, religionists simply point to Biblical passages in which human beings are commanded to love their neighbors as a matter of duty. It seems, however, for reasons indicated in the last chapter, that the development of benevolent attitudes and feelings has more to do with patterns of family and social life than with preaching or sermonizing. Certainly, parents who insist upon their child's duty to love them rarely receive the love they seek. Children may be persuaded that they ought to love their parents, but effort of will does not produce love. At best it produces lovelike behavior. And without an underlying spontaneous surge of good feeling the behavioral pretense is difficult to maintain and in most cases transparently artificial.

More sophisticated religionists, therefore, invoke the belief in the "fatherhood of God." The person who construes God as a father will, it is said, view fellow human beings as objects of benevolent concern, since the fatherhood of God entails the "brotherhood of man." What is at stake is not a mere command or moral imperative, but a deeply rooted attitude supported by a vast sum of religious symbolism and religious ritual. Once again, however, critics raise a question about the appropriateness of the family model as inspiration for moral relationships among adult human beings. For if the fatherhood of God implies the brotherhood of man, it also implies the childhood of brothers. Instead of direct ties of affection and identity among mature and autonomous individuals based on common, freely chosen programs and ideals, the family model carries with it a strong element of authoritarianism. Of course, those who feel that a strong authoritarian element is necessary to successful social living will not be disturbed by this. But those for whom individual autonomy and democratic equality are important ideals will find suspect any attempt to encourage love among human beings by cultivating a model of human relationships based on any kind of father figure.

Asceticism

Thus far in this chapter we have discussed moral claims made on behalf of religion and the criticism these claims have encountered. Now, we shall turn to three direct criticisms of religion. The first of these criticisms involves *religious asceticism,* or religiously motivated practices of self-denial. The more extreme manifestations of religious asceticism such as self-flagellation, pole sitting, and severe fasting are rare today. But there are many milder forms of asceticism that are not mere historical curiosities: life in conformity to the vows of poverty, chastity, and obedience required by many religious orders; the limitation of sexual intercourse to marriage; the Puritan work ethic; the Puritan rejection of pleasant diversions; and so forth. According to the critics, these practices are life denying and produce a great deal of wholly unnecessary suffering.

Criticism of religious asceticism is very old. In recent times the critics most frequently read are the nineteenth-century German philosopher Friedrich Nietzsche and Sigmund Freud. According to Nietzsche a religion that teaches ascetic self-denial is a religion fit only for slaves—for the tired, the weak, and the bitter. By denigrating human drives for self-expression those with a slave mentality manage to excuse their own weakness and to promote a smug sense of superiority over their betters, who delight in the full exercise of their human powers.

And according to both Nietzsche and Freud repressed human drives do not just disappear. Instead they are pushed back into the unconscious where they are distorted and removed from conscious direction and control. Thus, ascetic self-denial often produces not only useless frustration but also neurotic symptoms and morally reprehensible behavior. The frustrations of the sexually repressed, for example, often lead to resentment and malicious gossip against those with a healthy sex life. Even when basic human drives are predominantly antisocial, they should not be repressed but rather directed as well as possible into socially acceptable channels. In a famous essay called *The Moral Equivalent of War* the American philosopher William James elaborated upon this idea, suggesting that our more militant instincts need not be spent in killing one another but rather in a concerted drive to tame the forces of nature.

In addition to the unhappiness caused directly by the unhealthy repression of sexual and self-assertive drives, religion is charged with creating a great deal of unnecessary distress in the form of guilt. According to the critics the sense of guilt or moral regret is wholesome only if (a) it results from personal wrongdoing on the part of the agent and (b) it encourages a resolve to work for moral reform or betterment. But, the critics say, religious ascetics tend to take seriously the doctrine of original sin, according to which we are all sinners because of Adam's fall and share with him the responsibility for his disobedience. Clearly, this violates condition (a). Religious ascetics also tend to take seriously the related doctrine according to which the fall radically corrupted human nature, rendering us helpless to achieve good unless moved by divine grace. This doctrine is said to discourage efforts at self-reform and therefore violates condition (b).

A similar case is made with regard to suffering as a penance for sin. Punishment for moral wrongdoing is approved by the critics only as a tool in the process of moral education. The normal and legitimate goal of punishment is the formation of habits of right conduct in which the agent may take pride and from which society may benefit. But religious penance has a different goal: absolution, purification, or forgiveness. Penance is a religious act designed to humble the sinner and to propitiate God, not a part of a social process of moral educa-tion. Moreover, it presupposes the morally primitive notion of God as a tyrannical monarch who tolerates no rivals and who delights in undignified acts of homage from his subjects.

Religion and Rationality

As we saw in the last chapter, rationality is a crucial character trait. In its absence human beings blindly pursue immediate gratification at the expense of long-term well-being. Without it society cannot plan effectively and instruments of social control break down, since irra-tional behavior is wayward and difficult to predict. Without it ration-alization of self-interest and prejudice are the principal guides in moral deliberation. Moreover, other desirable character traits, such as benevolence and the sense of duty, lose much of their worth without rational guidance. Therefore, if religion tends to undermine rational-ity, as many critics of religion claim, the moral value of religion itself is greatly undermined.

To some extent what is involved here is the familiar conflict be-tween such findings of science as the Copernican hypothesis and evolutionary theory, on the one hand, and religious dogma, on the other. We saw earlier in this chapter how the scientific world view conflicts with the traditional religious world view. And for *fundamen-talists,* or those who believe in the literal truth of religious scriptures, this conflict is of crucial importance. Most religious groups today, however, have found some way of accommodating to scientific findings and are no longer greatly disturbed by the contradictions, be they real or apparent, between scientific knowledge and religious dogma. The real problem, as indicated earlier, is more basic. It has to do with acceptable methods of belief formation. The claim of religion's critics is that religionists in general tend to support nonra-tional methods of belief formation in religious matters and that these methods spill over into other areas of life, adversely affecting not only scientific progress but also public policy making, moral deliberation, and the practical decisions of everyday life. More specifically, the critics claim that religion strongly tends to support authority and faith as bases for belief at the expense of reason.

Although logic texts ordinarily list the appeal to authority as a fallacy, it is important to realize that not all appeals to authority are illogical or irrational. The student who consults a standard astronomy text to determine the distance between the earth and the moon is not committing a logical fallacy or making an irrational appeal to authority. The appeal to authority is irrational only if the authority in question has inadequate credentials. There is a story, probably apocryphal, according to which Voltaire on his deathbed was approached by a priest. Voltaire asked the priest who had sent him. The priest answered: "God." At this point Voltaire is said to have responded: "Your credentials, please." The point of this story is that critics of religion, if they are serious, do not condemn religion merely for its appeal to authority. The criticism must be that religious authorities, unlike competent scientists and historians, lack credentials that a rational person could accept.

Accordingly, our attitude toward religious authority depends on our position with respect to two issues: What credentials must a credible authority possess? And do religious authorities possess these credentials? The usual position with regard to the first issue is that an authority is worthy of belief only if there is evidence that all persons equally qualified in terms of intelligence, skill, education, and other similarly relevant factors would come to the same conclusions and would point to the same evidence in support of those conclusions. For example, we do have good reason for believing that any two intelligent people trained in the techniques of astronomical research would come to the same conclusion with regard to the distance that separates the earth and the moon. Moreover, authorities in astronomy tell us, and we have good reason for accepting their testimony, that their conclusions on this issue are based on the same evidence. In religious matters, however, the situation is altogether different. Alleged authorities on religious matters disagree regularly, and even those who do agree on a particular position often disagree about the basis for that position. Consider the many intelligent and educated people who have studied the question of God's existence. Some are believers, some are not. And among those who believe there is sharp disagreement about the nature of the supporting evidence. An argument that St. Anselm finds conclusive may be worthless in the eyes of St. Thomas. And not a few mystics who have based their belief in God on mystical experience have been declared heretics.

In dealing with religious faith we must be similarly careful in framing the issue. For not all forms of faith are irrational. As we all know, in matters of practical concern we rarely have the benefit of conclusive evidence. If the question is the trustworthiness of a friend or our ability to succeed in a project we have set for ourselves, we must normally rely on probable evidence. And where evidence is merely probable, there is always room for gnawing doubts. From time to time for various reasons still poorly understood those doubts assume irrational or neurotic proportions and pose problems that we would not encounter were our belief more properly proportioned to the strength of the evidence. We agonize, for example, about the support of friends whose loyalty has been successfully tested many times in the past, antagonizing them in the process. We allow irrational doubts about our abilities to paralyze us and ensure defeat. In cases like these we need more faith in the sense of belief from which irrational and neurotic doubts have been banished. And to the extent that religious faith is understood in this manner there can be no rational objection to it.

Usually, however, religious faith is not construed as a matter of banishing irrational doubts. Rather, faith is seen as a matter of belief in the total absence of evidence, the argument being that when there is no evidence either for or against a religious dogma we are free to believe on faith. Even St. Thomas, who is more or less the official philosopher of the Catholic Church and who assigned a greater role to reason in religious matters than most Christian philosophers, held that many crucial religious dogmas cannot be rationally demonstrated. Among these doctrines are the divinity of Christ, the creation of the world out of nothing, and the dogma of the trinity. Moreover, St. Thomas believed that large numbers of people could not appreciate the arguments in support of religious dogmas such as the existence of God and personal immortality, which he believed to be rationally demonstrable. Therefore, belief in the absence of evidence is often seen as appropriate even when evidence is available.

Often religionists congratulate themselves for believing on faith in the sense being discussed. They interpret their belief in the absence of evidence as an act of virtue. If there were evidence for religious doctrines, they say, their faith would be without moral merit. Moreover, in their eyes the fact that reason does not establish the falsity of religious dogmas means that belief in those dogmas is not irrational. And since they are persuaded that belief in religious dogmas has desirable consequences both for them personally and for society, they see religious belief as psychologically more wholesome and morally superior to nonbelief.

To this reasoning the critic makes two points. First, the opposite of belief is not disbelief, but suspension of belief. For example, if there is no evidence for the existence of God, both belief and disbelief are irrational. The rational response is suspension of belief. Rationality commands that we proportion belief to the strength of the evidence. If the evidence is strong, our belief should be strong. If the evidence is weak, our belief should be weak. And if there is no evidence at all, there should be no belief at all. If the chances that tomorrow's weather will be good for a picnic are exactly fifty-fifty, no rational person will decide to ignore the fifty percent chance that the weather will be unfavorable. Second, people who refuse to maintain an open mind on issues where the evidence is inconclusive, who authorize themselves to believe whatever they wish as long as there is no evidence to the contrary, are not in a position to make reliable judgments about much of anything. Certainly, they are not in a position to make reliable judgments about complicated issues such as the effect of religious belief on personal and social well-being. Childhood prejudice, social pressures, and psychological quirks bear so insistently on questions of this sort that only someone with a most scrupulous respect for rationality in all of its aspects can hope to see clearly.

Religion and Social Progress

The last criticism of religion we shall consider is succinctly summed up in the Marxist saying "Religion is the opium of the people." The usual interpretation of this saying is that religion discourages appropriate efforts toward social reform and social progress. Several common religious beliefs are held responsible.

In order to understand the relevant issues better it will be helpful to recall the discussion in Chapter One in which it was pointed out that in the face of injustice, suffering, or any other of the uglier aspects of life, there are normally two options available to the individual. One option is accommodation, or psychological adjustment. The individual learns to accept with equanimity things as they are. The other option is adaptation, or an active intervention in the situation designed to eliminate the evil. Instead of accepting things as they are the individual changes them. It was also pointed out in Chapter One that there are no hard and fast rules permitting us to determine whether accommodation or adaptation is appropriate in any given situation.

All we can say is that where it is possible to eliminate evils by human effort without introducing greater or equivalent evils in the process, adaptation is appropriate. Where this is not the case accommodation is called for. In the light of these observations this final criticism of religion can be restated. The criticism is that religion strongly encourages us to accommodate to social evils and human suffering when adaptation in the form of social change is called for.

One source of the tendency to accommodate to evil is said to be the religious conception of an all-powerful and loving God as creator of the universe. For if God is omnipotent, or all-powerful, and if God is also benevolent, or desires human good, then whatever is, is right. What we declare to be evils, the sufferings and injustices that appear to mar human existence, cannot really be evils despite appearances. They must be parts of a cosmic plan that viewed in its totality is good without qualification. Moreover, they must be borne with good cheer. An attempt to eradicate them would be fruitless, since it would come up against the omnipotence of God. It would also be impious, since it would exhibit an attempt on the part of a finite sinner to tamper with a plan imposed by an infinite and all-perfect being. As St. Paul said, and Luther after him, it is not right that human beings should attempt to overthrow an evil ruler. According to Romans, chapter 13, "the powers that be are ordained by God," and "whoever resists . . . resists the ordinance of God."

The religious attitude most frequently criticized as inimical to social progress, however, is called *otherworldliness*. Essentially, otherworldliness consists in the belief that there is a life after physical death and that our primary concern should be our fate in the world to come. Of course, by itself the concern for salvation after death is not incompatible with a concern for social improvement any more than a concern for one's own personal well-being is incompatible with a concern for the well-being of others. Conceivably, God might refuse salvation to those who are without a commitment to social progress. According to religion's critics, however, few religious authorities have related personal salvation to social commitment, and otherworldliness is almost always associated with religious views that lead us to ignore, minimize, or even oppose social progress.

One of the views associated with otherworldliness holds that those who suffer in this world will be more than compensated for their suffering in an afterlife. Jesus' Sermon on the Mount, in which he declared, among other things, that the first shall be last and the last shall be first, has often been interpreted in this way. Obviously, people who believe that a substantial sum of suffering in a short lifetime on earth will give them a preferred place for eternity in the world hereafter will not be greatly motivated to eliminate or reduce that suffering.

Another common view associated with the otherworldly outlook is that God intended our life on earth to be a "vale of tears," or a testing ground, in which we prove our fidelity to God through a patient acceptance of suffering. This has been said to be the message of the Biblical book of Job.

On still a third view, closely allied to asceticism, the earthly world is essentially evil and salvation is to be achieved not by changing it but by withdrawing from it. In fact, if human beings are basically evil, then a widespread satisfaction of basic human needs, which is the declared goal of those who seek social progress, could hardly be pleasing to God. Indeed, the idea of an earthly paradise or anything remotely resembling it to be achieved by human effort would strike those who believe in basic human depravity as a fruit of arrogant pride.

In closing this chapter we wish to remind the reader of the caution made at its beginning. Religion is very complex and many-sided, and few if any of the points raised here apply to all of the world's religions or even to all of the many traditions within any single religion. This should especially be borne in mind when considering the charges against religion developed in the last three sections of this chapter. Few contemporary religionists deny the existence of religious tendencies that could properly be attacked along these lines. But most regard these tendencies as distortions of true religion and argue that they are playing an ever less important role as religion evolves. Significantly, in many recent social struggles—for example, the civil rights movement in the United States—religious groups have often taken the lead or worked hand in hand with progressive political groups. How, many religionists ask, can the powerful deny the downtrodden their rights on earth if they know that God is prepared to give them a place in heaven?

Chapter 6

Right Conduct

Every society has a moral code—that is, a set of general rules that it enforces with moral sanctions. Those who observe the code ordinarily become respected members of their society and are encouraged to see themselves in a favorable light. On the other hand, those who violate the code are generally reproached by others and made to feel that they are without worth and dignity.

Although all moral codes require some degree of sacrifice, most people find it in their self-interest to live up to the moral code of their society. By definition a moral code is enforced by the external moral sanctions, and generally internal moral sanctions accompany and supplement the external sanctions. Also, violations of many moral rules, such as those prohibiting murder and slander, are punished with nonmoral sanctions, such as prison terms and financial penalties, as well as the moral sanctions.

Moreover, most people believe that society has a right to impose a moral code. As we saw in Chapter Two, humankind is a social animal in the sense that the good life requires a favorable social context. But human beings are not social animals in the way that ants and bees are social animals. Socially desirable human behavior is not genetically programmed, or instinctive. Socially desirable behavior must be socially encouraged. Society must set and enforce moral rules, just as it must set and enforce laws. The alternative is a Hobbesian state of nature in which everyone loses. Most people are aware of these facts, if only confusedly and half-consciously. As the French sociologist Émile Durkheim showed, the absence of a clearly enunciated and generally enforced moral code tends to produce a special form of individual disorientation and anxiety, to which he gave the name *anomie*.

Finally, most people believe not only that society has the right to impose a moral code but also that it has the right to impose just that code which in fact prevails. Most people inherit their moral code, as they do their religion. They do not choose it rationally after critical scrutiny.

No society, however, has ever secured full compliance with its moral code. There are two principal reasons for this. First, individuals are constantly tempted to violate the moral code in order to avoid the sacrifices it demands. No society has yet devised a set of external sanctions and instituted a process of moral education so perfect as to eliminate such temptations. Second, although most people clearly recognize the need for a moral code and tend strongly to accept the conventional code of their society, doubts about the validity of some of the rules figuring in that code do constantly arise. Moral rules that most people regard as legitimate social constraints are seen by others as forms of social oppression. Nietzsche argued that many of the moral rules of Christian societies express the resentment of ordinary people against those of superior talent and vitality. Marxists believe that some of the moral rules of capitalist societies are merely tools for keeping the masses down. John Dewey and Bertrand Russell opposed some of the moral rules of their day as outmoded customs or religious superstitions. And so forth.

These two reasons for noncompliance with the moral code are related. For the belief that a moral rule is legitimate is in itself an incentive for most people to observe it. On the other hand, the belief that a moral rule is illegitimate tends to make sanctions designed to ensure compliance less effective. The external sanctions, for example, often hurt less when one believes they are unwarranted. And, of course, the internal moral sanctions virtually cease to exist under these circumstances. If a homosexual reared to believe that homosexuality is wrong comes to believe that it is not wrong, there may be occasional lingering guilt feelings but by and large the new belief wipes out these negative internal sanctions. Nonetheless, the question of justifying moral rules is distinguishable from the question of securing compliance, and in this chapter our primary concern will be with the first of these questions.

Moral Relativism

We shall use the term *moral skepticism* here to refer to the view that disagreements about the validity of a moral rule cannot be rationally resolved even in principle. In saying that reason cannot resolve this kind of disagreement even "in principle" the intent is to exclude the possibility that the problem is merely a practical or temporary one—that it is due, for instance, to lack of knowledge that may some day be forthcoming. The idea is that the nature of moral disagreement is such that reason could never cope with it.

Moral skepticism takes several forms. One of these is called *moral relativism*. According to this view the final authority for any moral rule is not reason but the society that happens to support and enforce it. When we say that a certain type of behavior is "morally right" all we can possibly mean is that some society approves of it and positively sanctions it. If a second society says that the same behavior is "morally wrong" and negatively sanctions it, then that behavior is right in the first society and wrong in the second. There is no universal, or cross-cultural, morality.

Although moral relativism has many adherents, it does not seem to have any firm or clear theoretical basis. Most relativists simply give examples of actual moral differences among various societies, apparently assuming that if there were a rational method for resolving moral disagreements this method would by now have eliminated these disagreements. The possibility that a rational method exists but has not been discovered or properly applied is not given serious consideration. Sometimes, relativists merely lump moral judgments together with other value judgments and contrast these with factual or scientific judgments. Differences on factual or scientific issues, they argue, are resolvable, as the history of scientific progress shows. Value judgments, on the other hand, cannot be rationally justified, since in this area there is no history of progress.

No one, of course, disputes the fact that different societies have different moral codes. Anthropologists disagree about the extent of moral disagreements among different cultures, but none denies the existence of cross-cultural disagreements. Similarly, some people believe that there has been a measure of progress in the direction of moral agreement, but everyone agrees that there has been greater progress in scientific matters than in matters of value. The question, therefore, is whether these facts justify the claim that reason cannot even in principle resolve moral differences.

Opponents of relativism usually make some combination of the following points:

1. Most moral views reflect social pressures and elicit passionate allegiance. The difficulty of resolving moral issues, therefore, is better explained not by reference to some inherent limitation of reason but rather as a consequence of the fact that passion and social prejudice often cause us to reject the authority of reason. Whether the earth is round or flat, for example, is a matter of fact, not a matter of value. Yet those who have been reared in a society where the earth's flatness is proclaimed as a religious truth often resist rational argument here no less than when confronted with a moral issue. Similarly, whether there is an international conspiracy of Jewish bankers and financiers is a factual, not a moral, issue. Yet anti-Semites are notoriously reluctant to heed the voice of reason where this point of fact is concerned. In other words, to understand why moral progress has been relatively slow the distinction we need is not the distinction between fact and value but rather the distinction between issues—be they factual or moral—that involve passion or social prejudice and issues that are free of these complications. Reason has no less authority in the realm of values than in the realm of facts.

2. Even if questions of moral value are not directly susceptible to rational resolution, many of them are indirectly subject to rational resolution. For disagreements about particular moral rules usually presuppose differences of opinion with respect to questions of fact. For example, cannibalism often rests on the factual belief that eating the flesh of the enemy is necessary to the survival of the group; human sacrifice in religious ritual, on the factual belief that there are angry gods who will be placated by the sacrifice; the burning of witches, on the factual belief that there is a Devil and that human beings make pacts with the Devil; and so on.

3. Almost all of the progress in factual and scientific matters has taken place in the last few centuries, and so far it has been almost wholly restricted to the physical sciences such as physics, chemistry, and biology. Most of the social sciences, from which moralists would naturally expect the most help, have come into existence only within the last century. To take the absence of progress in settling moral questions as a basis for skepticism about the possibility of rationally resolving them, therefore, makes little sense. It would be as if someone

in the sixteenth century denied the possibility of progress in the physical sciences simply because modern science had not yet gotten off the ground.

4. Where science has come into conflict with socially indoctrinated prejudices, science has tended in the long run to overcome these prejudices and there has been a movement toward cross-cultural agreement. Few people today still believe that the earth is flat. To take another example, before the advent of modern science there was an amazing variety of nonscientific, usually religious, views about the origin of humankind. Today evolutionary theory tends to prevail almost everywhere in the world among educated people as the favored theory about the origin of the human species. If the social sciences make progress and begin to produce findings as authoritative as those of the physical sciences, one can expect a similar overcoming of moral prejudices and a similar movement toward cross-cultural agreement.

5. As already noted, the fact that cross-cultural moral differences exist does not in itself justify the belief that no rational method exists for resolving such differences. The fact could also be explained as a result of prejudice, emotional blocks, ignorance, or a misuse of appropriate rational methods for establishing moral rules. There is, however, still another explanation for many cross-cultural differences. Moral relativists often assume that if a moral rule could be rationally certified as valid in any one society, it would have to be valid in any other society. If, for example, a moral rule such as "One ought not to commit polygamy" had a rational warrant, it would have to have universal validity. This assumption is closely related to a second—namely, that if reason is competent to pass on moral rules, moral rules must be universal truths of the same kind as "Columbus discovered America in 1492." Obviously, this latter statement cannot be true in one society and false in another. But opponents of relativism have questioned these assumptions. Could it not be that historical and cultural differences would rationally warrant different moral rules in different societies? Suppose, for example, that one is a utilitarian, believing that the ultimate justification of any moral rule in any society is its tendency to produce the greatest happiness for the greatest number. Is it not conceivable that reason or science would show that in society A polygamy works better than monogamy, whereas in society B monogamy works better than polygamy? In other words, the fact of differing moral rules in different societies may often be due to perfectly rational assessments of differing social needs.

Subjectivism and Emotivism

Another form of moral skepticism is called *subjectivism*. According to the subjectivist the final authority for any moral rule is neither reason nor society but individual feeling. The individual who says that a certain kind of behavior is morally right is simply stating a personal preference. A statement of the form "X is right" is equivalent to a statement of the form "I, the speaker, approve of X." If, therefore, Jones approves of X while Smith disapproves of X, the statement "X is right" is true when uttered by Jones and false when uttered by Smith.

Closely related to subjectivism is a view sometimes called *emotivism,* and sometimes called the *expressive-directive theory.* This theory, like subjectivism, holds that the final authority for the correctness of a moral utterance is individual feeling. On this second view, however, a moral utterance does not state, or assert, a truth of any kind, not even a truth about the speaker's feelings or likings. Since sentences of the form "X is right" are grammatically similar to sentences such as "X is blue" or "X is six feet tall," the subjectivist mistakenly concluded that "X is right" must also be used in the same way: to provide information or to assert a truth. But in spite of their grammatical form sentences like "X is right" do not give information and cannot therefore be true or false. They are more like an exclamatory sentence such as "Alas!" or an imperative sentence such as "Close the door," neither of which is intended to give any information and neither of which is said to be either true or false. The function of moral sentences is not to *assert* how one feels but to *express* one's feelings and to influence the behavior of others. When a mother tells a child "Children should be seen and not heard," she is not communicating a truth or imparting an item of knowledge. She is rather expressing her impatience and directing the child to keep quiet. Gestures could have served the same purpose.

Like relativism these other two forms of moral skepticism have a fairly large number of adherents. Moreover, most subjectivists and emotivists tend to argue for their view by stressing the lack of progress in the direction of moral agreement and the differences between matters of fact and questions of value. The criticisms of relativism cited above, therefore, also apply to subjectivism and emotivism. To deal adequately with the latter theories, however, it is necessary to raise a number of additional issues regarding the nature of moral judgments.

First, let us look more carefully at the differences between the relativists, on the one hand, and the subjectivists and emotivists, on the other. The relativists say that the purpose of a moral code is to express the will of society. Thus, a moral rule such as "Smoking marijuana is wrong" is equivalent to something like the following: "Most people in this society disapprove of smoking marijuana and impose moral sanctions against those who do." This second statement is a factual statement that may be either true or false. If it is true, the person who says "Smoking marijuana is wrong" is warranted in making the statement. According to the subjectivists and emotivists this analysis of moral utterances is false. Suppose that you live in a society where most people disapprove of smoking marijuana but that you personally approve of it. In this case you would be misleading others if you said "Smoking marijuana is wrong." For others would infer from your saying "Smoking marijuana is wrong" that you personally disapprove of it. And to say "Smoking marijuana is wrong, but I approve of it" is very much like saying that something is both round and square at the same time. Thus, the right to say that smoking marijuana is wrong depends not on what society in general feels but on what each of us individually feels. Almost all philosophers today agree with the subjectivists and emotivists on this point. Moral judgments regularly reflect the feelings, likings, or attitudes of the speaker, and it is an abuse of language to say that something is morally wrong if you individually approve of it or to say that something is morally right if you personally disapprove of it.

But from the fact that the presence of an appropriate personal attitude of approval or disapproval on the part of the speaker is a necessary condition for the making of a moral judgment it does not follow that it is a sufficient condition. To say appropriately and correctly "Smoking marijuana is wrong" you must disapprove of it. But simply because you disapprove of smoking marijuana it does not follow that you are entitled to condemn it morally, or call it wrong. For just as the expression of a moral judgment implies an appropriate attitude of the speaker toward the object of that judgment, so also it implies that the speaker believes the object of the judgment to have certain traits, or characteristics—often called *right-making characteristics* or *wrong-making characteristics*—that justify the speaker's attitudes. A simple expression of personal taste such as "I dislike spinach" can, indeed, be justified by the mere presence of an appropriate subjective reaction. But a moral rule is not a mere expression of personal taste and must be justified by showing more than an appropriate subjective reaction. The person who says "Smoking marijuana is wrong" but is unable to tell us what it is about smoking marijuana that makes it wrong has misled us. Just as the rules of ordinary usage forbid us to say that something is wrong unless we disapprove of it, so they forbid us to say that something is wrong unless we are prepared to defend that judgment by citing wrong-making characteristics. Moral language is not to be used lightly. If we merely wish to give vent to our feelings, there are many ways of doing so without using moral language. And the fact that we do use moral language means that we must be prepared to accept a challenge to defend the attitude expressed. "X is wrong, but I have no reason for thinking so" is hardly less misleading than "X is wrong, but I approve of it."

It is for this reason that almost no professional philosopher today accepts subjectivism or emotivism in the crude and simplified versions stated above. In the more recent and sophisticated versions of the subjectivist-emotivist tradition most moral judgments are seen as serving two purposes. First, they are said to express the speaker's subjective attitudes and desire to influence the behavior of others. This is said to be their *emotive meaning,* or *expressive-directive meaning.* Second, they are said to imply that the speaker is prepared to defend the use of moral language by citing right-making or wrong-making characteristics. The right-making or wrong-making characteristics implied by the use of moral language are said to constitute the *descriptive meaning* of moral judgments. Accordingly "Smoking marijuana is wrong" has emotive meaning insofar as it reflects an attitude of disapproval toward marijuana and a desire to influence others to stop smoking it. The judgment also has descriptive meaning insofar as it implies the presence of wrong-making characteristics that justify the speaker's attitude of disapproval and the use of the word "wrong."

Clearly, then, most moral skeptics today do not deny that reason has a role to play in the resolution of moral disagreements. Many moral disputes revolve around the presence or absence of alleged wrong-making or right-making characteristics. For example, most disagreements about marijuana turn on such questions as whether marijuana is in fact injurious to health and whether marijuana smoking does really lead to a dependency on hard drugs such as heroin. These beliefs are factual beliefs, and although we may not have enough information now to determine their truth or falsity, it is undoubtedly within the province of reason to settle these questions. Any difficulties that exist are difficulties in practice, not in principle. Similarly, many disagreements about capital punishment turn on factual questions such as: Does the threat of capital punishment deter crime? How often are innocent people executed? Does the fact that the state permits itself to take a life encourage private citizens to do the same? Does the penalty of capital punishment fall most heavily on the underprivileged? And so forth. And there can be no doubt that if science gave us clear answers to these relevant factual questions, many moral disagreements about capital punishment would be resolved to the satisfaction of the parties concerned. Contemporary moral skepticism, therefore, is less radical than skepticism in the past.

Contemporary moral skepticism also takes a different form. Its chief tenet today is that many differences of opinion about what constitutes a relevant factual issue, or what characteristics count as right-making or wrong-making characteristics, are not resolvable by reason.

Let us elaborate. Moral rules have different levels of generality. For example, the rule "One ought to be kind" is more general than the rule "One ought to help the blind at street corners." Moreover, many of the less general rules are subordinate to others in the sense that they are instances, or specifications, of those others. "One ought to help the blind at street corners," for example, is not only less general than "One ought to be kind" but subordinate to it insofar as helping the blind at street corners is an instance of kindness. A less general rule that is subordinate to some other is called a *lower-order rule;* the rule to which it is subordinate, a *higher-order rule.*

Normally we justify lower-order rules by showing that they are instances of higher-order rules. We accept the rule about helping the blind at street corners *because* it is an instance of the rule about kindness, because helping the blind at street corners has kindness as a right-making characteristic. And if the rule ever came into question any factual issues bearing on the kindness or lack of kindness in helping the blind at street corners would be considered relevant. Similarly, if the higher-order rule itself came into question we would determine what factual considerations are relevant by reference to some still higher-order rule to which it is in turn subordinate. Clearly, however, this justification of one rule by showing that it is an instance of a higher-order rule cannot go on forever. At some point we must come to an *ultimate moral principle*—that is, a highest-order rule that is not subordinate to any other. At this point, so the argument goes, the process of rational justification must come to a halt. We cannot justify ultimate moral principles by an appeal to facts because we do not even know what facts are relevant. As a final court of appeal in decisions regarding what is to count as a right-making or a wrong-making characteristic, an ultimate moral principle cannot itself be justified by an appeal to such characteristics.

Of course, if two parties to a dispute happen to have only one ultimate moral principle and that principle is the same for both parties, there is no special problem. If, for example, the two parties are both utilitarians, then the utilitarian principle constitutes a common basis for discussion and will be a satisfactory court of last appeal with regard to what is a relevant factual issue. But if one of the parties subscribes to the utilitarian principle and the other, say, to the theological principle, there is no longer a common basis for discussion. The one who subscribes to the utilitarian principle will insist that the crucial factual considerations have to do with social utility whereas the one who subscribes to the theological principle will insist that they have to do with the will of God.

This contemporary skeptical argument can be stated in a different way. There is general agreement that ultimate moral principles are, in effect, definitions of right conduct. The utilitarian, for example, believes that a right act is by definition one that promotes the greatest happiness of the greatest number. And if that definition is rationally acceptable, then all moral disputes are in principle capable of rational resolution. Given rational agreement on that definition, establishing a moral code becomes wholly a matter of determining what does and what does not accord with the definition, just as determining whether a physical substance is a piece of gold depends on determining whether it has the defining properties of gold. More specifically, given a utilitarian definition of "right" and "wrong," lower-order moral rules of the form "X is right (wrong)" become equivalent in descriptive meaning to statements of the form "By virtue of certain right-making (wrong-making) characteristics X does (does not) promote the greatest happiness of the greatest number." And statements of this second kind are factual statements that may in principle be established as true or false and therefore fall within the province of reason. But, say the skeptics, definitions of moral terms cannot be justified on a rational basis Whether, for example, we accept or reject the utilitarian principle does not depend on what we believe to be the case but rather on how we feel. If we care about the greatest happiness of the greatest number, we will tend to accept it. If we do not care, we will reject it. Feelings alone determine how we define moral terms.

Thus, the subjectivists and emotivists, who in response to criticism abandoned the view that lower-order moral rules can have no rational foundation, nonetheless persist in affirming that ultimate moral principles can have no rational foundation. The person who utters an ultimate moral principle is simply asserting or expressing a feeling, an attitude of approval or disapproval, and attempting to influence the behavior of others. These are the only possible functions of ultimate moral principles. No rational considerations may be advanced to favor one ultimate moral principle over another.

It might be thought that the crucial issue here is whether ultimate moral principles may be construed as true or false. As we saw, by virtue of ultimate moral principles lower-order moral rules become implicit assertions to the effect that something possesses certain right-making or wrong-making characteristics. As such, lower-order moral rules may be true or false, and it is because of this that reason is relevant to the resolution of disagreements about these rules. Ultimate moral principles, however, are not implicit assertions of this sort. If ultimate moral principles are to be construed as assertions of any kind, they must be seen as assertions about the correct use of moral terms. In other words, their truth or falsity, if either of these terms applies, must be of the kind that pertains to definitions. But it is generally recognized that there is only one kind of definition that may be properly characterized as true or false. This kind of definition, called a *reportive definition,* consists of a report on the way in which a term is actually used. It is also generally recognized that in presenting an ultimate moral principle we are not merely reporting on how a word is used. Utilitarians, for example, do believe that there is a close association in the popular mind between the idea of right conduct and the idea of social utility and that this fact ought to count in favor of the utilitarian principle. But in saying that a right act is by definition one that promotes the greatest happiness of the greatest number, they are not merely saying that most people do as a matter of fact use the term "right act" in this way. They are urging everyone, including those who use the term "right act" differently, to adopt their definition. In other words, ultimate moral principles are not reportive definitions but rather *recommendatory definitions,* or definitions proposed for adoption by others. The crucial issue with regard to ultimate moral principles, therefore, is not whether they can be meaningfully regarded as true or false. Almost all moral philosophers agree that they cannot be so regarded. Recommendatory definitions, like other recommendations or proposals, may be good or bad, well-founded or ill-founded, but not true or false.

Nor does the controversy turn on the general possibility of rationally justifying recommendatory definitions, or definitions that cannot be evaluated as true or false. Although one of the important functions of reason is to pronounce on issues where truth or falsity is at stake, it is widely agreed that reason has other functions, including that of approving or disapproving recommendatory definitions in the sciences. For reason is not merely the faculty by which truth is discovered. It is also the faculty by which we select the most appropriate means to the achievement of our goals. And since recommendatory definitions in the sciences are best considered tools designed to aid in the achievement of scientific goals, it is for reason to decide whether these tools are well chosen. The decision to define the word "fish" nonreportively in terms of anatomical properties rather than in terms of natural habitat and to define physical substances nonreportively in terms of atomic number rather than color or weight were rational in the fullest sense of the term. And no one has even suggested that current scientific controversies over different proposed, or recommended, definitions of light cannot even in principle be resolved by reason.

The crucial issue, therefore, is whether definitions of ethical terms have peculiarities that not only distinguish them from definitions in the sciences but that at the same time put them beyond the pale of rational evaluation. The moral skeptics believe that moral definitions do have such peculiarities.

One of these alleged peculiarities of ultimate moral principles is, of course, their emotive, or expressive-directive, force. Scientists who urge the adoption of a particular definition of fish, for example, do not have any feelings of approval or disapproval toward fish or toward the characteristics they want accepted as defining traits. But ultimate moral principles, like all moral judgments, do involve feelings of approval or disapproval. Therefore, if one person proposes the utilitarian principle and a second person the theological principle, the issue is simply the sincerity of their feelings. If the person proposing the utilitarian principle genuinely feels that the final test of the rightness of an act is its social utility and if the person proposing the theological principle genuinely feels that the final test is the will of God, then each is entitled to the respective ultimate moral principle and neither would be entitled to adopt the other. The reply here is once again that the moral skeptic has simply taken a necessary condition for a sufficient condition, thereby repeating the error originally made with regard to moral rules. Indeed, the adoption of an ultimate moral principle would be illegitimate if the agent did not have the appropriate attitude of approval, but the presence of an appropriate attitude of approval does not of itself make the adoption legitimate.

We come, therefore, to a second alleged peculiarity of moral definitions. As we saw, scientific definitions are rationally defended by showing that they serve well certain goals or aims that are common to members of the scientific community. But, say the skeptics, ultimate moral principles are intended for human communities, and human communities do not have any shared set of goals that could be furthered by the adoption of one moral principle to the exclusion of others. The person who advocates the theological principle has one set of goals, and the person who advocates the utilitarian principle has a different set. Moreover, these respective principles, insofar as they are *ultimate* moral principles, reflect the ultimate goals of the respective parties. There is, therefore, no common overarching set of goals that would provide a common frame of reference for evaluating different ultimate moral principles.

The rejoinder here is that ultimate moral principles are ultimate only in the sense that they constitute a highest-order rule within a system of hierarchically ordered rules. The attitudes or feelings that these principles reflect are not necessarily ultimate in the sense that all other attitudes or feelings are psychologically subordinate to them. And even if they were, it would not necessarily follow that these "ultimate" attitudes or feelings could not be modified as a result of rational deliberation and a better understanding of one's self and one's society.

Besides, it is better to join the issue posed by this second alleged peculiarity of moral definitions at a less general and abstract level. The fact is that ultimate moral principles are generally expected to serve three specific and concrete purposes. (1) Almost everyone believes that most of the prevailing moral rules have some characteristic in common that most people are prepared to accept as a good reason for observing them. An ultimate moral principle is expected to make explicit the nature of that common characteristic and thereby reinforce adherence to the moral rules. (2) Although most people accept without serious question the majority of the conventional rules and expect an ultimate moral principle to justify them, there are more or less serious questions about a few of the conventional rules and ultimate moral principles are expected to help in resolving these questions. (3) Moral rules often conflict with each other. To take a prosaic example, we often have to choose between being kind and telling the truth. Most of us expect ultimate moral principles to help us to decide how we ought to behave in such cases.

Surely, say the nonskeptics, there is no good reason for thinking that reason cannot even in principle evaluate the relative merits of proposed ultimate moral principles in terms of the adequacy with which they fulfill these three functions.

The Utilitarian and Other Ultimate Moral Principles

So far we have had a number of occasions to bring up the utilitarian principle (according to which a right act is one that promotes the greatest happiness of the greatest number) and the theological principle (according to which an act is right if it accords with the will of God). Throughout most of the Christian era the theological principle prevailed, but since early in the nineteenth century, under the influence of Bentham and Mill, utilitarianism has gained rapidly in favor not only among moral philosophers but also in popular thinking.

Let us first examine the theological principle. As we saw in Chapter Five, many people believe that those who adopt the theological principle thereby become enmeshed in a vicious logical circle. (Readers who do not clearly recall that argument may refresh their memory by referring back to page 129.) There are still other major criticisms of the theological principle. First, the principle presupposes a factual claim—namely, the existence of God—that many people dispute. Obviously, those who do not believe in God do not believe that moral rules have the right-making characteristic of being in conformity with God's will. Second, if the evidence for God's existence is inadequate, then there is no rational basis for the religious incentives to right conduct and the theological principle fails reliably to motivate adherence to the moral code. Third, even if God existed and we were in fact rewarded for behavior in accordance with the divine will, we would need some satisfactory way of determining what the divine will is. But according to critics of the theological principle, there is no satisfactory way of determining God's will. Except in closed societies where religious dissent is not tolerated, religious authorities regularly disagree. If, therefore, the validity of a particular moral rule comes into question or if two moral rules come into conflict, the theological principle is of little, or no, help in resolving the problems thereby posed.

As already indicated, the utilitarian alternative to the theological principle is in general more congenial to the contemporary mentality. And it does appear better to fulfill the functions expected of an ultimate moral principle. It calls attention to the fact that most conventional moral rules have social utility—a fact that is not in serious dispute. And to the extent that we care about the welfare of others or recognize the importance of a stable and harmonious social order to our personal well-being, the utilitarian principle does give us a good reason for conforming to the moral code. Moreover, although there are serious problems in connection with the definition of happiness and great practical difficulties in determining the consequences of human behavior, the utilitarian principle does provide in principle a rational basis for resolving disagreements about the legitimacy of any given moral rule and for resolving problems that arise when moral rules conflict.

Despite widespread sympathy with its general thrust, the utilitarian principle has been subjected to considerable criticism. There is, in fact, general agreement today that this principle is unacceptable without substantial refinements, clarifications, or modifications. Moreover, many people do not believe that utilitarianism can be satisfactorily patched up. There are still advocates of the theological principle. And a number of philosophers—most notably John Rawls—favor an approach to many moral issues, especially those relating to individual rights and distributive justice, in terms of social contract theory rather than along utilitarian lines.

One relatively minor problem turns on an ambiguity in the utilitarian principle that went virtually unnoticed in the days of the classical utilitarians. This ambiguity concerns the term "right act." Ordinarily, the person who says a right act promotes the greatest happiness of the greatest number is interpreted to mean that we have a moral duty, or obligation, to do whatever promotes the greatest happiness of the greatest number. And it appears that Bentham and Mill intended to equate the morally right act with the morally obligatory act. But on reflection most of us recognize a number of acts that are morally right but not morally obligatory—that is, meritorious acts over and beyond the call of duty. These acts are called *acts of supererogation*. No one, for example, is morally obliged to be a martyr or a hero in battle, but acts of martyrdom and heroism may be not only right but superlatively right, "more right" than acts merely in conformity to duty. Moreover, most utilitarians would want to say that acts of supererogation are right by virtue of their social utility just as morally required acts are. Accordingly, the utilitarian formula must be qualified so as to indicate which of the acts that promote the greatest happiness of the greatest number are morally required and which are supererogatory. Otherwise, the utilitarian formula misleadingly lumps together two very different kinds of morally right acts.

A second, and much more serious, criticism turns on the claim that the utilitarian principle has consequences that offend our sense of justice and our feelings about the rights of individuals. Suppose, for example, that a sheriff has in custody a man accused of a vicious murder. The sheriff knows that the man is innocent, but the jailhouse is surrounded by an angry mob convinced of the man's guilt and determined to lynch him. Suppose further that the situation is such that unless the sheriff turns over the innocent man there will clearly be a riot in which many people will die. Consider a second case, posed by Dostoevsky in *The Brothers Karamasov*. In this case God has offered humankind a bargain. In return for turning over an innocent child whom God will cruelly torture eternally, the rest of humankind will receive eternal bliss. According to the critics, in these and similar cases the utilitarian principle would require the sacrifice of the innocent individual. But since this sacrifice is clearly unjust, there must be something wrong with the principle itself.

Those who oppose utilitarianism on this basis are attacking what is called the *teleological view of ethics,* or *consequentialism*—according to which the concept of duty, or right conduct, is logically subordinate to the concept of good. In other words, the teleologists, who are most conspicuously represented by the utilitarians, claim that right conduct must be formally defined as conduct that leads to the good. By definition conduct is morally right only if its consequences are good. The opposing position is called the *deontological view,* or *nonconsequentialism.* The deontologists argue that although right conduct does generally have good consequences, this is not always or necessarily so. Some conduct is morally right even though its consequences are bad. We cannot, therefore, define right conduct as conduct with good consequences.

The first, and still the greatest, of the major deontological philosophers is Kant. According to Kant moral rules—or "moral maxims," as he preferred to call them—are best viewed as commands, laws, or imperatives. And according to him moral imperatives are not *hypothetical imperatives*—that is, they are not to be obeyed because of desired or desirable consequences. Rather, they are imperatives that must be obeyed because of their very nature or content without regard to possible consequences. The moral command to abstain from lies, for example, is not like a recipe for a cake or an instruction accompanying a do-it-yourself assembly kit, which we can follow or ignore depending on how we happen to feel about the end to be achieved. Rather, according to Kant, it is a law of practical reason with universal validity. In the last analysis, says Kant, an act is right if and only if the maxim, or rule, to which it corresponds has universal validity. The only legitimate ultimate moral principle, therefore, is what Kant called the *categorical imperative:* "Always so act that the maxim of your action may be willed as a universal law."

Few people today accept Kant's categorical imperative. Many persons, however, sympathize with Kant's contention that moral rules have universal validity, or admit of no exceptions. And it is especially on this point that the classical utilitarians have been attacked by many of their contemporary critics.

To see the issue more clearly, it is necessary to elaborate on our discussion of utilitarianism. According to most interpreters, the classical utilitarians like Bentham and Mill advocated what is today called *strict utilitarianism,* or *act utilitarianism.* According to this view, valid moral rules are rules of thumb based on past experience. Past experience shows that in ordinary circumstances observing these rules leads to the greatest happiness of the greatest number. But past experience also shows that from time to time circumstances arise in which observance of a moral rule does not have its ordinary consequences and actually impedes the achievement of the greatest happiness of the greatest number. Under such circumstances the rule not only may but must be broken. More often than not cases in which we are required to violate a moral rule are cases in which the rule to be violated conflicts with another rule. An example given earlier is that in which we must choose between telling the truth or being unkind. However, many different kinds of unusual circumstances might require violation of a moral rule. The essential point of act utilitarianism is simply that moral rules are not universal laws and do admit of exceptions.

To designate their own view, which upholds the need for a utilitarian justification of moral rules and simultaneously the universality of moral rules, a number of contemporary critics of classical utilitarianism have adopted the terms *rule utilitarianism* or *limited utilitarianism*. Most rule utilitarians do not give elaborate theoretical arguments against act utilitarianism. They tend rather to present cases such as those cited earlier in which their sense of justice or respect for individual rights would be outraged if a decision were made according to what they consider to be the dictates of act utilitarianism. They say that act utilitarians are too quick to modify their sense of right and wrong in particular cases in the light of their ultimate moral principle. Act utilitarians are accused of forgetting that one of the major tests of the legitimacy of an ultimate moral principle is the extent to which the principle justifies our sense of right and wrong in particular cases. Surely, if some proposed ultimate moral principle turned out to justify murder or rape we would know for that reason alone that the principle was defective. Similarly, the fact that the utilitarian principle would lead us to condemn an innocent person to death is a sufficient reason for rejecting it.

There was, however, one interesting attempt to give rule utilitarianism theoretical underpinnings. John Rawls, who was strongly attracted to rule utilitarianism early in his career, claimed that the act utilitarian view of moral rules as rules of thumb based on past experience is unduly simplistic. Rawls argued that at least some moral rules —for example, the rule against breaking promises—are like the rules of a game. Thus, the act utilitarian who says there is a moral rule against breaking promises but that under unusual circumstances it can be set aside would be like a baseball player who says: "There is a rule according to which each batter in baseball has three strikes, but under unusual circumstances I may have four." The rules of baseball define the game of baseball. If one does not adhere to the rules, one is simply not playing the game. Likewise, some moral rules help to define the practice of morality. To claim exemptions is to abandon the practice of morality altogether.

There is, however, a significant difference between the rules of a game and the rules of morality. The rules of a game such as baseball are all consistent with one another. The rule providing for nine innings, for example, does not conflict with the rule allowing for exactly three strikes. Moral rules, on the other hand, do conflict. Consider, for example, the doctor who must break a promise—for example, a promise to have dinner with a friend—in order to save a patient who is critically ill. The rule utilitarian, therefore, appears to be in the position of asking us to do the logically impossible: to observe moral rules even when they conflict.

Kant seems not to have faced this problem squarely. Consider a case that Kant himself posed. A man who falsely believes that a third party has wronged him comes to us asking about the third party's whereabouts. He does so, he makes clear, with the intent of locating and killing the third party. Are we, Kant asks, allowed to tell a lie under these circumstances? For most of us this problem is not very difficult. There is, we would say, a moral rule according to which we must prevent senseless killings. There is also a moral rule according to which we must not lie. The first rule, however, for utilitarian reasons takes priority over the second. We are not only permitted to tell a lie in these circumstances but are actually under a moral obligation to do so. Kant, however, cannot analyze the situation in this way. All moral rules are inviolable. Even in the circumstances described it is wrong to tell a lie, he says. But what about the rule to prevent senseless killings? On this Kant is silent.

Rawls for his part once argued that properly formulated moral rules cannot conflict because properly formulated rules incorporate a list of standard situations in which exceptions are permitted. For example, the general rule against lying would, if properly formulated, contain a provision that permits lying in order to save someone's life. But there is something odd about making rules exceptionless by stating the allowable exceptions. Indeed, it is difficult to see how we could determine what exceptions should be allowed without, in effect, admitting that moral rules conflict. If, for example, we say that we should incorporate in the moral rule against lying an exception when someone's life is at stake, are we not implying that there is a moral rule urging the preservation of life and that this rule has priority over the moral rule against lying in the event of conflict?

Act utilitarians have not been content, however, merely to point out what they take to be weaknesses in the deontologists' theoretical views. Many act utilitarians have also been troubled by the kinds of cases deontologists cite to show the inadequacy of act utilitarianism. With regard to these cases they tend to make one or more of three observations.

1. All or nearly all of the cases in which strict utilitarianism appears to imply a disregard of the principles of justice or individual rights are imaginary, or hypothetical, cases that would never occur in real-life situations. And it is simply unreasonable to expect anyone to come up with an ultimate moral principle that will not only serve the practical functions expected of such a principle in real-life situations but also resolve any kind of moral dilemma that anyone with sufficient leisure can manage to think up. An ultimate moral principle that serves us well in the real world is good enough. We do not need a principle that would serve us in any possible world such as that odd world in which God offers humankind peculiar bargains.

2. A particular violation of a moral rule almost always has two negative consequences. First, it tends to weaken the agent's habitual tendency to act in accordance with the rule and thereby to jeopardize the agent's excellence as a being of moral worth. It is a commonplace that each lie told makes subsequent lies easier. Second, the violation of any moral rule tends to undermine the social fabric and to introduce an element of instability into the social world. As we have noted several times, widespread confidence in the general observance of moral rules is a necessary condition of social well-being. But both of these negative consequences of particular violations of moral rules must according to act utilitarianism itself be taken into account when attempting to determine the legitimacy of any particular violation. And when these negative consequences are taken into account, most real-life situations that at first appear to require a violation of justice or individual rights under act utilitarianism appear in a different light. For example, the sheriff who is tempted to turn over the innocent man to the angry mob should ask himself what will happen to his personal integrity if he does so and what will happen in the long run to public faith in the administration of justice. Having done so, he may well decide that the situation is not a simple matter of one life or many lives and that the innocent man must be protected for the sake of the greatest happiness of the greatest number in the long run.

3. When deontologists present cases in which act utilitarianism appears to demand an injustice to an individual, almost invariably the case is incompletely described. The plight of the individual who is negatively affected by a decision in accordance with act utilitarianism is poignantly described and immediately elicits our sympathy. The plight of the people negatively affected by the decision is not even mentioned or is allowed to remain comfortably in the background. We

are encouraged, for example, to visualize dramatically the lynching of the man falsely accused but we are not asked to consider the cruel deaths of equally innocent persons in the riot that would erupt if he were not turned over to the mob. According to its defenders, one of the great merits of act utilitarianism over rule utilitarianism lies precisely in the fact that act utilitarianism encourages us to take all of the circumstances and everyone's interests into account when we act. Rule utilitarianism, on the contrary, encourages us to apply rules mechanically without sufficient regard for all of the circumstances and all of the people affected.

Closely related to the problems with utilitarianism raised by deontologists is a problem posed by a second ambiguity in the utilitarian formula—which, like the ambiguity pointed out earlier, went virtually unnoticed in Bentham's and Mill's day. As we all know, happiness cannot be measured with mathematical exactitude, and it is often difficult to know how many courses of conduct are open to us in any given situation or how many people our choices affect. But to illustrate the ambiguity in question let us suppose that we face a choice between exactly two courses of conduct, that each of these two courses of conduct affects exactly four persons (the same persons in each case), and that we can assign numerical weights to the happiness or unhappiness of these persons as a result of each of these choices. Let us further suppose that the results of our calculations are as indicated on the following table.

	Course A	Course B
Person 1	+ 2	+ 10
Person 2	+ 2	+ 3
Person 3	+ 2	− 3
Person 4	− 3	− 3
Totals:	+ 3	+ 7

If we adopt Course A, three persons are made happy instead of only two and we thereby produce happiness for a greater number of persons. But if we adopt Course B, we produce seven units of happiness rather than three, or a greater total sum of happiness. If, therefore, we put the stress on that part of the original utilitarian formula that speaks of happiness for "the greatest number" Course A is indicated. If, however, we stress "the greatest happiness" Course B is indicated.

Otherwise stated, the problem is as follows: The original utilitarian formula clearly implies that in deciding on a course of behavior we must take the interests of everyone affected into account. But it does not tell us whether our duty is to promote the greatest possible sum of happiness without regard to its distribution or whether we should be concerned not only about the total sum of human happiness but also about its distribution. Nor, of course, if distribution is taken into account, does the formula give us any idea as to the weight that should be accorded to broad distribution.

There are differing views about the practical importance of this ambiguity. Some people feel that the extent of mutual interdependence in human communities is such that situations in which we could produce the greatest possible sum of happiness by disregarding its distribution must be practically nonexistent. These people simply cannot envisage a happy person in the midst of an unhappy community. At the opposite extreme, however, there are those, like Nietzsche, who claim to see enormous differences in human capacities and who argue that the elite may flourish only if the masses are condemned to a dull and impoverished existence.

If, then, we should be confronted with a choice between a policy that promotes a greater total sum of happiness to be enjoyed by relatively few and a policy that promotes a smaller total sum of happiness to be distributed among a greater number of persons, what should we do?

Although Nietzsche did not raise this problem in these terms, it is clear that he would favor the greater total sum of happiness for the few at the expense of the many.

Most philosophers today, however, feel strongly that a broad distribution of goods is important in its own right and must often be promoted even at the cost of a greater total sum of happiness. And some—John Rawls, for example—have argued that no social policy is just unless it is to the advantage of everyone. To sacrifice A for B's benefit violates A's individual rights. But because Rawls saw no way of justifying this conviction on classical utilitarian grounds and because he was unsatisfied with his earlier attempts to construct a rule utilitarian theory, Rawls developed a social contract theory. According to this theory, rational individuals in a state of nature drawing up a social contract would never agree to any social policy unless everyone, including especially the most disadvantaged, benefits from it. It would be irrational to run the risk of being victimized by a policy according to which some people gain at the expense of others.

However, the contemporary American philosopher Robert Nozick—who, like Rawls, sees in classical utilitarianism a threat to individual rights—disagrees with Rawls on this point. According to Nozick if policies affecting the distribution of wealth must work out to everyone's advantage, then it would be necessary to abandon such basic individual rights as the right to dispose of one's property as one sees fit—for example, by giving it away or trading it for something else. Nozick claims that a proper respect for individual rights requires that policies affecting the distribution of wealth be formulated without regard to their consequences. Instead of looking forward and asking what pattern of distribution we would like to establish, we should look backward and ask how present-day accumulations of wealth were acquired. Nozick has, therefore, proposed a new theory of distributive justice, called the *entitlement theory*. On this theory persons are entitled to the goods they actually hold if these goods have been acquired according to principles of justice covering (a) the original acquisition of holdings, (b) the transfer of holdings, and (c) the rectification of injustices in the original acquisition or transfer of holdings. Unfortunately, Nozick has not spelled out in any detail the nature of these principles of justice. It is clear, however, that Nozick believes that they would authorize individuals to acquire holdings without regard for the welfare of disadvantaged individuals or groups and would permit "other capitalist acts between consenting adults."

There is one more major criticism of utilitarianism. As indicated near the beginning of this discussion, the utilitarian principle does call attention to a characteristic of most moral rules that most people take to be a good reason for adhering to them. In particular, benevolent people, who have a personal interest in the welfare of others, find in the social utility of a moral rule a reason for observing it. And so do people who, whether benevolent or not, recognize that a society in which happiness is generally maximized is likely to be one that improves their own individual chances of happiness. But many critics of utilitarianism say that this is not enough. What of the person who does not personally care about the welfare of others? What of the person who fails to appreciate the extent to which individual happiness depends on the general good? And what about those particular cases, which everyone knows from personal experience, where the personal benefits of observing a moral rule are outweighed by personal losses? No one is so morally perfect and no one's personal happiness is so utterly dependent on general social well-being that it will always be in that person's interests to promote the greatest happiness of the greatest number.

Two assumptions are implicit in this criticism. First, there is the assumption that "a good reason" for observing moral rules must be a reason that actually motivates people to observe those rules and that a fully satisfactory ultimate moral principle must ensure full compliance with the moral code it justifies. Some people have rejected this first assumption, arguing that it is enough for an ultimate moral principle to appeal to rational people or to people of good moral character. But if we agree that ultimate moral principles are recommendatory definitions and if we agree that the adequacy of such definitions depends on how well they serve the functions intended, it is difficult to see how this assumption can be so easily rejected. For, clearly, in addition to helping us resolve conflicts of interest and helping us determine the acceptability of disputed moral rules, a recommended ultimate moral principle is also expected to provide an incentive for widespread observance of the moral code.

Nonetheless, there is something very utopian, even absurd, in the expectation that any verbal formula, no matter how crucial it may be to a moral system, could ensure one hundred percent compliance with the moral code it justifies. The only nonutopian and reasonable expectation is that a proposed ultimate moral principle satisfy the functions such principles are intended to serve better than alternative proposals. And if the utilitarian principle does satisfy these functions better than the theological principle, it does constitute a milestone on the road of moral progress.

The second assumption implicit in the criticism under discussion is that to secure compliance with the moral code an ultimate moral principle must appeal to the agent's self-interest. This assumption is based on a doctrine known as *psychological egoism,* according to which it is psychologically impossible for those who believe that an act is contrary to their self-interest voluntarily to perform that act. This doctrine is very old. Plato, like other Greek and Roman philosophers of the classical period, took it for granted that if adherence to the moral code is not in the agent's self-interest the agent has no good reason to observe it. Supporters of the theological principle throughout most of the Christian era also tended to take psychological egoism for granted. That is why so many of them despaired of securing adherence to moral rules in the absence of divine sanctions after death. Nothing, many of them argued, but the self-interested hope in eternal rewards and the self-interested fear of eternal damnation could keep us to the straight and narrow path of virtue.

Today psychological egoism is not so widely accepted as in the past, although much of the current controversy over this issue is marred by a failure to distinguish between a narrow, crude definition of self-interest and a broader, more adequate definition that takes into account the personal satisfactions and dissatisfactions that accompany internal sanctions like benevolence and conscientiousness. When the broader definition is adopted, however, psychological egoism does not seem unduly cynical. Some people may from time to time act voluntarily in the knowledge that their behavior is contrary to their best all-round, long-range interests. If one looks into the lives of saints and heroes one may find examples of such acts. But it is hardly deniable that the vast majority of people do regularly act on what they take to be their own self-interest broadly defined. If, therefore, the term "self-interest" is broadly defined, an ultimate moral principle is unlikely to serve as a generally effective incentive to right conduct unless it appeals to self-interest. And to the extent that an ultimate moral principle fails as an effective incentive it is apparently deficient.

The utilitarian could argue, however, that when individuals do not find it in their interest to observe the utilitarian code, the fault is not with the utilitarian principle itself but rather with the imperfect implementation of the principle. For if it is in the general interest that a moral rule be generally observed, it is also in the general interest that a society make it in the interest of individuals to observe the code. In other words, the rules of any fully adequate utilitarian code must include rules for the enforcement of other rules. And when individuals find it in their interest to violate some rule, there is a great likelihood that the rules for the enforcement of rules have not been properly formulated or implemented. By way of illustration, if social utility dictates a rule against lying, it also dictates that lying be actively discouraged. If, therefore, a child lies with impunity, experiencing neither the remorse of a bad conscience nor an external penalty, we should not worry about the legitimacy of our ultimate moral principle. Rather, we should worry about parents, teachers, and the community as a whole. Either they have failed as moral educators or they have failed to create a social environment in which honesty is indeed the best policy.

Punitive Justice

As we pointed out in the introductory comments to this chapter, the reasons for noncompliance with a moral rule are of two different sorts. First, it may be that the person who violates the rule does not accept its legitimacy. Possibly the agent disagrees with society about some relevant factual issue. Possibly the agent believes that the rule is incompatible with some higher-order rule. Possibly the rule follows from an ultimate moral principle that the agent believes to be without rational foundation. Second, an individual may violate a moral rule, even while accepting its legitimacy, for lack of proper motivation. Perhaps the external sanctions are insufficient or inappropriate. Perhaps the agent has been imperfectly socialized, or received an inadequate moral education—that is, lacks the required degree of rationality, benevolence, conscientiousness, or some other morally desirable character trait.

In this section we shall assume the legitimacy of the moral code and turn to the question of motivating observance of the code. We shall not, however, address ourselves to all major aspects of the question, most of which have been dealt with in earlier chapters. Instead, we shall focus on only one part of the general question: When are we entitled to use negative sanctions, or to punish, someone? This question is often referred to as the question of *punitive justice,* or *corrective justice,* to distinguish it from the question of distributive justice, discussed in Chapter Two. The question of punitive justice may be posed with regard to internal moral sanctions. When, it may be asked, is it appropriate to feel guilt or moral regret for one's behavior? Punitive justice also relates to the law. When, for example, should persons be fined, or imprisoned, for a violation of the law? Here, however, we shall be primarily concerned with punitive justice so far as the external moral sanctions are concerned, our question being: When should society use negative external moral sanctions such as blame to punish violations of moral rules? For the most part, the kinds of considerations that are relevant here are also relevant in the other cases.

The clearest and in the twentieth century the most widely accepted (though still highly controversial) theory of punitive justice is that of the act utilitarians, who argue that a particular case of punishment is just if and only if it will produce the greatest happiness of the greatest number. More specifically, since every act of punishment by definition involves some pain or unhappiness for the person being punished, an act of punishment is right if and only if the balance of good over evil is greater as a consequence of this punishment than it would be if there were no punishment. Still more specifically, since an act of punishment is likely to produce a greater balance of good over evil only if the punishment deters future violations of the rule in question, an act of punishment is just only if it has a deterrent effect. Thus, the position on punitive justice taken by most utilitarians is known as the *deterrence theory of punishment.* If an act of punishment tends to deter the agent from future violations of the rule, it is said to be *reformative* or *rehabilitative.* If an act of punishment tends to deter people other than the agent, it is said to be *exemplary*—that is, it serves as a warning, or example, to others.

In practice it is often difficult to know whether a particular act of punishment will have a deterrent effect. There are, however, a number of standard circumstances in which a deterrent effect is unlikely. And those who hold to the deterrence theory take comfort in the fact that most people do not generally blame people under these circumstances.

First, there are cases in which an agent is acting under a physical handicap or a psychological compulsion. Nobody blames a cripple for failing to save someone from drowning. Nor do we ordinarily blame a compulsive alcoholic for overindulgence. In order for an act to be blameworthy it must be one which the agent could do or refrain from doing as a result of a personal choice or desire. But neither the cripple's desire to save the drowning person nor the compulsive alcoholic's resolve to quit drinking has any bearing on actual conduct. In the case of the physical cripple the ineffectiveness of choice is obvious. And if the alcoholic is truly compulsive, it is equally clear in this case, since by definition the difference between a noncompulsive and a compulsive drinker is that the former can stop simply by choosing to do so whereas the latter cannot.

Second, there is a tendency to withhold blame whenever the agent violates a moral rule without awareness that a violation is being committed. For example, someone might violate the rule of kindness by unintentionally saying something that offends a stranger. Since this act does not express a malicious disposition that blame might curb, blame does not serve the same useful purpose that it would had the offensive comment been maliciously intended. Blame, therefore, is inappropriate. Of course, the offensive comment though unintentional may have been tactless and blameworthy on this account. But then again the comment may have been offensive only because of unusual circumstances that the agent could not reasonably be expected to have known. The essential point is that blame is unlikely to deter the repetition of a wrongful act insofar as the act is a consequence of unavoidable ignorance or accident.

Finally, we do not ordinarily blame someone for wrongful behavior when the behavior is motivated by some desirable character trait. If, for example, people perform a wrongful act because it is in accord with some moral rule that they mistakenly believe to be legitimate, we would not ordinarily blame them. The habit, or disposition, of acting in conformity with what one believes to be legitimate moral rules has great social utility, and we would not like to endanger or weaken that habit by blaming an agent so motivated even when we know that the agent is wrong about the legitimacy of a particular rule. Of course, if the belief in the illegitimate rule is a consequence of some failure of rationality on the part of the agent, we might want to take the agent to task for imperfect rationality. But the culpable behavior in this case is not the agent's action in conformity with what the agent regarded as a legitimate rule but rather the failure to submit the rule to rational examination.

Although, as indicated earlier, our primary focus in this section is on punishment, it is worth noting that the utilitarian principle of deterrence as a criterion for punishments has a counterpart in the principle of reinforcement as a criterion for rewards. As we have just seen, for the utilitarian the usual purpose of punishment is to deter the repetition of wrongful acts by counteracting antisocial habits, or dispositions, that motivate these acts. Likewise, for the utilitarian the usual purpose of praise is to encourage the repetition of rightful acts by reinforcing socially useful habits, or dispositions, that motivate these acts. Suppose, for example, that two persons make equal contributions to some charity. Suppose, further, that the situations of these two persons are alike in all relevant respects except that the first has a long history of giving to charities whereas the second does not. Which of these persons should receive the greater praise? Obviously, the first is more admirable since this person has a long-established habit of giving whereas the second does not. But precisely because the first has a well-established disposition to give, praise is not likely to be useful. In all probability, this person will continue to give whether praise is received or not. The second person, however, needs praise as a stimulus, or encouragement, to further giving. The habit of giving is weak and must be reinforced. Therefore, praise is more common and because of its greater utility more appropriate in the second case.

In other words, although goodness of moral character and praise-worthiness generally go together, they do not always go together. Given a utilitarian theory of justice morally inferior persons may often be more praiseworthy than their moral superiors. And it is probably the failure to appreciate this point that leads many people to assume that a benevolent giver is morally inferior to a nonbenevolent giver and to define the unselfish person as one who gives without any personal reward of any kind. (See Chapter Four, p. 106.) The benevolent giver *is* a morally superior, or more admirable, person than the nonbenevolent giver. But this will not be immediately apparent to someone who confuses the concepts of moral goodness and praiseworthiness.

The principal rival to the deterrence theory of punitive justice is known as the *retributive theory of punishment*. According to the retributionists justice requires that every transgression of a legitimate moral rule be punished and that the punishment be proportioned strictly to the gravity of the offense. The question of a useful social purpose should simply not arise at all. The Biblical phrase "an eye for an eye and a tooth for a tooth" is often invoked to express the spirit of the retributive theory. This view of punishment is obviously a deontological view, and like most deontological views it is usually supported less by theoretical argument than by inviting us to consider cases that allegedly illustrate the shortcomings of the teleological approach. Insofar as a theory does lie in the background of the re-tributive position, the theory seems to be that every offense to the moral code upsets a delicate balance in a cosmic moral order that can be restored only by the suffering of the offender. It is as if the appropriate degree of suffering by the offender had a weight equal to the weight of the offense and therefore returned the cosmic scales of justice to a state of equilibrium.

Critics of the retributive theory usually dismiss the tendency to see justice as a matter of a moral order in equilibrium. As a poetic metaphor "the scales of justice" may have a certain appeal. But it is worthless as a tool for philosophical analysis. The problem of punitive justice is one of determining how best to use punishment in order to create a better and happier society. For obvious reasons social utility itself demands that offenses usually be punished and that the severity of the punishment correspond roughly to the gravity of the offense. But since punishment is the deliberate infliction of suffering by some on others, it is inhumane to use punishment automatically and without a careful regard to its consequences on each occasion of use. Exceptions under circumstances of the kind mentioned earlier must be recognized. And this is not simply a matter of tempering justice with mercy. For there is no greater injustice than the unnecessary infliction of suffering upon others. Moreover, if the antisocial tendencies that motivate a given offense could be corrected as well or better by the use of positive sanctions, or rewards, these positive sanctions should become the primary means of moral education. Punishment, if used at all, would be merely an auxiliary device.

In addition to fighting off attacks from the retributionists utilitarians have also had to fight off attacks from those who oppose all punishment whatsoever. Those who argue that punishment is never warranted usually start from the widely accepted premise that blame and other forms of punishment are appropriate for a given act only if the agent is free to perform or not to perform that act. But, they go on, no one is ever free. Everything is determined. We may for lack of sufficient knowledge not understand the causes of an individual's behavior, but science and common sense both presuppose that a causal explanation exists and that in principle it could be discovered. In the last analysis individual behavior must be explained in terms of heredity and environment. Since we are not masters of our fate, we are not genuinely responsible for our behavior. No one, therefore, ought to be punished.

Some philosophers have responded to this view by arguing that although some human behavior is indeed caused, or determined, some human behavior is uncaused, or undetermined. Accordingly, our moral responsibility, or liability to blame, is limited to those acts that are uncaused. This position is known as *libertarianism*. There is, however, a strong objection to libertarianism. It was forcefully stated by the eighteenth-century British philosopher David Hume. According to Hume if an act were uncaused there could be no moral responsibility for it. The idea here is that in order to hold somebody morally responsible for an act we must know its underlying motive, which is at least in part a cause. For only if we know the motive are we in a position to determine whether punishment will serve a useful purpose. Suppose, for example, that a husband kills his wife, and there is no ascertainable motive for his behavior. To all appearances the husband

and wife were mutually devoted and happy together. There had been no quarrel. There was no insurance to be collected or property to be inherited. There was no third party in the picture. And so forth. Would we not withhold judgment until we had more knowledge? How could we determine the likely effect of punishment under these circumstances?

The utilitarians have, therefore, tended to endorse a second and more widely accepted answer to those who argue for the inappropriateness of all punishment. This answer is based on a distinction between a free act in the libertarian sense of an uncaused act and a free act in the sense of an act that is uncompelled, or unconstrained. This distinction was also made by Hume. Hume's point is that in order for agents to be morally free and morally responsible, their behavior must be uncompelled, or unconstrained, but need not be undetermined. For example, an alcoholic who suffers from a psychological compulsion to drink is not morally free or morally responsible. To blame a compulsive alcoholic would be a useless act of cruelty, since it would serve no useful purpose. But from this it does not follow that alcoholism is uncaused. On the contrary, we have good reasons for believing that compulsive alcoholism does have causes and that it can be treated by eliminating those causes. On the other hand, a nonalcoholic—that is, someone who is not under any compulsion to drink and who could execute a decision not to drink—is free to stop drinking and is morally responsible for overindulgence. In this case blame could serve a useful purpose, and it could serve that purpose even though we had a full causal explanation of the nonalcoholic's drinking patterns. The view that determinism and moral responsibility are not mutually exclusive is frequently called *compatibilism*.

Underlying the deterrence theory of justice is a distinctive conception of morality in general as an enterprise, or task, to be achieved— namely, the task of devising and securing compliance with a set of rules so that human beings may live together more peaceably and happily. Accordingly, the test of any moral rule or practice is whether it works in human experience, whether it enriches or impoverishes our lives. This conception of morality has pervaded many currents of thought during the nineteenth and twentieth centuries, not only the utilitarian but also the pragmatist and socialist traditions. Historically, however, throughout most of the Western tradition going back to antiquity, morality was conceived largely as a matter of discovering eternal and absolute truths. The ultimate touchstone for evaluating moral rules and practices was some reality beyond human experience such as the will of God or the cosmic scales of justice. Whether in the long sweep of history the newer view will finally prevail is one of the crucial questions of our day.

Discussion Questions

In the author's experience these questions have generated lively classroom exchanges. Some oblige the students to examine critically ideas presented in the text. Some oblige the students to use ideas presented in the text to analyze aspects of their personal experience or to explore concrete moral problems. They are not review questions; answers will not usually be found in the text. In fact, only a very few have "right answers" in any ordinary sense of that expression. And individual students cannot be expected to do much with these questions without the help of classmates and the instructor. In my opinion the value of posing questions such as these consists not merely in any resulting enlightenment with regard to the specific issues raised. Of equal value is the tendency of these questions to generate a greater awareness of the need for more relevant factual knowledge and the exchange of opinions in the development of enlightened moral views.

CHAPTER ONE
The Good Life

1. In the last section of this chapter, five elements in personal well-being are listed. Have others been overlooked?

2. What are the greatest sources of unhappiness in your own life? To what extent are you personally responsible for these sources of unhappiness? To what extent are social conditions responsible?

3. Have parents, teachers, or others taken the time to talk with you about the nature of the good life? Do you think that high schools ought to find a place for this question in the required curriculum?

4. Many American states have laws against "unnatural" sex acts. On the whole do such laws increase or diminish the sum of human happiness?

5. It is often said that we should all fulfill our potential. Is this saying unduly simplistic? Why or why not?

6. In the text the point is made that many people have a tendency to take refuge from the past or future by living as exclusively as possible in the present. Do you think that significant numbers of people also tend to take refuge in the past or in the future, failing to give due importance to the present? Does age bear on this question?

7. Have you ever had to abandon some ambition or goal because of adverse circumstances? Was it more or less difficult than you anticipated? How exactly did you manage it?

8. It is sometimes said that those who devote great time and energy to the task of better adapting the basic structure of their society to fundamental human needs forfeit personal happiness in the process. The happy person is presumed to be someone who takes the basic social structure for granted as something to which he or she must accommodate. Do you agree? Why or why not? (In dealing with this question it might be helpful to keep in mind important historical figures. For example, did Che Guevara have a good life?)

9. What is the relationship between money and happiness? Does the need for money vary from one person to another, from one culture to another? Is there a point beyond which more money is of little or no importance? Is money important to a good self-image? Under what circumstances?

10. Do you think that satisfying personal relationships are easier or harder to form in later life? Why?

CHAPTER TWO
The Good Society

1. What are the six major social goals discussed in the text? Have others of equal importance been overlooked? If so, what are they?

2. What is the relationship between social instability and unpredictability? What unpredictable circumstances in your own life give you the greatest anxiety? What social changes might help to make those circumstances more predictable and alleviate your anxiety?

3. What are the two principal ways in which society attempts to create greater social harmony? Which, if either, of these two strategies is generally to be preferred? Why?

4. It has been said (by Samuel Johnson) that patriotism is "the last refuge of a scoundrel." Do you agree or disagree? Why?

5. On what basis, if any, can "reverse discrimination" be justified?

6. From what you know about the distribution of wealth in the Soviet Union and in the United States, in which society is wealth more justly distributed? Why?

7. Explain the difference between freedom from restraint and freedom of choice without using the term "freedom." Do you think that freedom of choice is secondary? Why or why not?

8. What is meant by legal freedom? moral freedom? material freedom? What is the basis of this classification of types of freedom? Which of the three types of freedom is most important? least important? Why?

9. What do you think of the expression "the free world"? In what sense, if any, are capitalist countries generally more free than socialist countries? In what sense, if any, are the socialist countries more free than the capitalist countries?

10. Is material well-being primarily an intrinsic or an instrumental good? Do you think Americans in general tend to overemphasize material well-being? Why or why not?

CHAPTER THREE
Good Government

1. The United States' Bill of Rights accords U.S. citizens "the right to bear arms." Why might this right have been considered important at the time the Constitution was adopted? Can it be defended today? Is it "inalienable"?

2. In capitalist societies "the right to work" often means the right of a worker to accept a job without joining a union or at lower than union wage rates. In socialist societies "the right to work" usually

means that every citizen who wishes to work has a constitution-ally guaranteed right to a job. Which use of the term do you prefer? Why?

3. What are your principal activities? How many are strictly private —that is, without any direct or indirect effects on others?

4. What is meant by "the work ethic"? Are you for it or against it?

5. In Cuba many foods are in short supply. Some people argue that this is evidence of the failure of socialism. Do you agree? Explain your reason for agreeing or disagreeing.

6. Socialists often maintain that capitalist nations are forced to maintain huge and wasteful defense establishments because disman-tling these establishments would seriously disrupt their economies. Is this argument sound?

7. How important would worker control over the work process be to the happiness of the worker? Does worker control tend to reduce economic efficiency? If so, is reduced economic efficiency a price worth paying?

8. The term "democratic education" has at least three different meanings: (a) student government, (b) preparation for citizenship in a democratic society, and (c) unrestricted admissions policies. Should all schools be democratic in all three of these senses? Why or why not?

9. What is the proper role of elected officials in a democratic society? Should they be merely instruments of the will of the majority or do they have a responsibility to help shape the will of the majority? What should they do when they believe that the interests of the nation as a whole conflict with the interests of the segments of the population they represent?

10. The founding fathers of the United States tried to prevent the abuse of political power by a system of checks and balances—among the executive, legislative, and judicial branches of government and also between the federal government and the state governments. How well has this system worked? Could this or a similar system help to prevent abuses of power in a socialist society?

CHAPTER FOUR
Good Character

1. Can you think of socially valuable character traits other than those discussed in the text?

2. Do the people you know who pride themselves on being individualists use the word "individualism" in the same sense as it is used in the text? If not, how do they use it? Is the kind of individualism denoted by alternative uses of the term a good thing? Why or why not?

3. Many people think that the most important single factor in the development of good character is the example set by "role models" —that is, persons whom the individual comes to respect or admire and, therefore, emulate. Do you agree or disagree?

4. To what extent do you think the American Revolution was a consequence of idealism? Do you think the colonists' use of violence to achieve their goals was justified? To what extent do you think the French, Russian, Chinese, and Cuban revolutions were a consequence of idealism? Do you think the use of violence in these cases was more or less justified than in the case of the American Revolution?

5. Do you think that intelligence and education are in general favorable or unfavorable to the development of good moral character? Explain.

6. It has been said that the ways of the world are such that the wicked prosper and the virtuous suffer. Is this true or false? If it were true, would parents be justified in educating their children to be morally good?

7. Is the social climate of the United States excessively competitive? What forms of competition do you favor preserving? What forms would you like to see eliminated or reduced?

8. Many people have said that it is better to work within the system than to attempt to change it. What moral issues, if any, are involved here?

9. Foreign observers have frequently said that Americans are a self-indulgent people, always intent on instant gratification. Is this charge true? If so, what should be done about it?

10. Since the time of de Tocqueville, in the middle of the nineteenth century, foreign observers have accused Americans of being excessively conformist. Is this charge true? If so, what should be done about it?

CHAPTER FIVE
Religion and Morality

1. How much truth, if any, do you think there is in the claim that a moral breakdown has occurred in the last century as a result of the decline of religion? If you think there has been a moral breakdown can you think of possible nonreligious causes for it?

2. In your opinion what are the most praiseworthy causes for which human beings have fought in the last two centuries? Was the inspiration for these movements largely religious or secular?

3. Is the separation of church and state a good thing? Why or why not?

4. Atheists often say that religious believers use religion as a crutch. The believers often counter by saying that atheists are merely acting out some kind of adolescent rebellion against parents or society. What measure of truth, if any, is there in these accusations? If one of these claims were substantially true, would this have any bearing on the truth or falsehood of religious doctrines?

5. Religionists often accuse atheists of pride insofar as they attempt to get along on their own resources without help from God. Atheists often accuse religionists of pride for thinking that they are in a position to know that God exists and to instruct others about the nature of God's commands. What merit, if any, is there in either of these accusations?

6. Many Christians say that Jesus died for the sins of humankind. What are the moral implications of this view?

7. In the Old Testament it is said that Abraham was prepared to kill his son Isaac because he believed that this was God's command. What are the moral implications of this story?

8. St. Thomas distinguished between natural, or secular, virtues and

"theological," or religious, virtues. Do you see any sound basis for this kind of distinction? (For St. Thomas the four cardinal virtues of the Greeks—wisdom, courage, justice, and moderation—are natural virtues. The theological virtues are faith, hope, and love.)

9. Much of the world's great art has been inspired by religion, and many people regard religious ceremony and ritual itself as a particularly high form of art. Would the level of artistic experience necessarily be lower in a purely secular society?

10. Jean-Paul Sartre, the French existentialist, does not believe in the existence of God. He has said, however, that God's existence would be irrelevant to morality, since human beings are by nature free and free beings must choose their own values. (This theme is illustrated dramatically in Sartre's play *The Flies*.) Do you agree or disagree with Sartre on this point? Why or why not?

CHAPTER SIX
Right Conduct

1. What does it mean to say that moral judgments are "relative"? To what are they relative? In what ways? Are all moral judgments relative to the same things and in the same ways?

2. What kinds of value judgments are there? How do other value judgments differ from moral judgments?

3. Many people argue that anomie—the absence of a clearly enunciated and generally enforced moral code and the consequent psychological disorientation of the individual—is one of the greatest ills of our time. Do you agree or disagree? What bearing does this question have on the view according to which children need discipline and suffer from too much permissiveness?

4. It is often said that "the end does not justify the means." What moral view does this saying express? Do you agree with it?

5. Can you think of moral disagreements to which differences in factual beliefs are irrelevant? How many moral disagreements would be unresolved even if all underlying factual disagreements were resolved?

6. It is often said that the major differences between socialists and capitalists are moral rather than factual. Do you agree or disagree? Why?

7. Most utilitarians believe that the social utility of negative moral sanctions consists entirely in their deterrence value. Do you agree or disagree? What about the social utility of imprisonment and capital punishment?

8. Psychological egoism is a doctrine about the behavior of individuals. What about social classes or groups? Do they ever act in ways that they believe to be contrary to their own interests? Try to think of historical examples. How often do social classes or groups act to their own disadvantage because of avoidable ignorance, prejudice, or some other failure of rationality? Again, try to think of historical examples.

9. What does the expression "moral absolutes" mean to those who use it? Do you think it is a useful expression?

10. Under what conditions would you say that a moral rule is legitimate? Under what conditions would you say that it is illegitimate?

Suggested Readings

In the listing of suggested readings the usual bibliographical data has been omitted in the case of books that exist in several readily available editions.

CHAPTER ONE
The Good Life

Hedonism. Of the writings of Epicurus only fragments are extant. The best introduction to his views is the long poem *De Rerum Natura* by Lucretius, a famous Roman writer of the first century B.C. The best introduction to Jeremy Bentham is his *The Principles of Morals and Legislation;* to John Stuart Mill, *Utilitarianism.* For Bentham's hedonistic calculus see Chapter Four of *The Principles of Morals and Legislation.*

Life According to Nature and Self-Realization. This tradition was initiated by Aristotle, whose moral views received their classic statement in the *Nichomachean Ethics.* Two twentieth-century versions of this position, reflecting the influence of St. Thomas Aquinas, are Jacques Maritain, *The Rights of Man and Natural Law* (New York: Charles Scribner's Sons, 1943) and Mortimer J. Adler, *A Dialectic of Morals* (Notre Dame, Indiana: University of Notre Dame Press, 1941). A modern and influential view showing the influence of the self-realization theorists is that of Abraham Maslow, *Toward a Psychology of Being* (Princeton, New Jersey: Van Nostrand Reinhold, 1962).

One of the few major twentieth-century philosophers to deal specifically with the concept of happiness is Bertrand Russell, *The Conquest of Happiness* (New York: Liveright, 1958).

CHAPTER TWO
The Good Society

There is a vast literature dealing specifically with distributive justice and freedom. The other social ideals discussed in Chapter Two—stability, harmony, cohesion, and material prosperity—have rarely been dealt with separately and at length. As a rule positions on these social goals are merely implicit in larger overall views regarding the nature of the good society. In the Western tradition the most influential overall social philosophies are those of Plato in the *Republic* and Thomas Hobbes in *Leviathan.* Sigmund Freud's *Civilization and Its Discontents* raises interesting questions about the psychological effects of social restraints. Russell Kirk, *The Conservative Mind* (Chicago: Henry Regnery Company, 1953) presents a typical conservative view of the good society in the tradition of Edmund Burke, an eighteenth-century English statesman and thinker often called the father of conservatism. Joel Feinberg, *Social Philosophy* (Englewood Cliffs, New Jersey: Prentice-Hall, 1973) is a short book intended especially for college students.

Distributive Justice. Richard Brandt, ed., *Social Justice* (Englewood Cliffs, New Jersey: Prentice-Hall, 1962) is an anthology giving a good idea of the wide range of positions on this question. R. H. Tawney, *Equality* (New York: Capricorn, 1961) is a well-known work by an English historian with socialist leanings. Chapter Five of John Stuart Mill's *Utilitarianism* is a classic statement of the utilitarian view of justice. Nicholas Rescher, *Distributive Justice* (Indianapolis, Indiana: Bobbs-Merrill, 1966) is a sympathetic but critical examination of the utilitarian view.

Freedom. Dostoevsky's *Legend of the Grand Inquisitor* is a part of his novel *The Brothers Karamasov* but it has been published separately in several editions. See also Dostoevsky's *Notes from the Underground.* The two works have been published together in a translation by Ralph Matlaw (New York: E. P. Dutton, 1960). The most brilliant technical statement of the existentialist theory of freedom is found in Jean-Paul Sartre, *Being and Nothingness,* a difficult book. Isaiah Berlin, *Four Essays on Liberty* (Boston: Beacon Press, 1969) is a highly readable book by an eminent political and social philosopher. The essay "Two Concepts of Liberty" is especially well-known. Robert E.

Dewey and James A. Gould, eds., *Freedom: Its History, Nature, and Varieties* (New York: Macmillan, 1970) is a comprehensive anthology. B. F. Skinner, in *Beyond Freedom and Dignity* (New York: Alfred A. Knopf, 1971) argues for the inevitability of social controls over the individual. Skinner's *Walden Two* (New York: Macmillan, 1948) is an earlier but still classic statement of the same theme.

CHAPTER THREE
Good Government

Individual Rights. John Locke's views on the social contract and inalienable natural rights are found in his *Two Treatises of Government.* John Rawls, *A Theory of Justice* (Cambridge: Harvard University Press, 1971) is a highly distinguished contemporary continuation of this tradition. For a brief statement of Rawls' position see "Justice as Fairness," *The Philosophical Review,* Vol. lxvii (April 1958). Robert Nozick, *Anarchy, State, and Utopia* (New York: Basic Books, 1974) is a strong contemporary defense of the minimal state. The classic utilitarian defense of limited government and guaranteed individual rights is in John Stuart Mill's *On Liberty.* For the view that capitalism favors individual rights see Friedrich A. Hayek, *The Road to Serfdom* (Chicago: University of Chicago Press, 1963) and Milton Friedman, *Capitalism and Freedom* (Chicago: University of Chicago Press, 1962). For a criticism of this view see C. B. Macpherson, *Democratic Theory* (Oxford: Clarendon Press, 1973), especially pages 143–156; Robert Paul Wolff, *The Poverty of Liberalism* (Boston: Beacon Press, 1968); and Alan Wolfe, *The Seamy Side of Democracy: Repression in America* (New York: David McKay, 1973).

Capitalism and Socialism. For a contemporary defense of laissez-faire capitalism see Ayn Rand, *Capitalism: the Unknown Ideal* (New York: The American Library, 1967). Leo Huberman and Paul Sweezey, *Introduction to Socialism* (New York: Monthly Review Press, 1968) presents a traditional Marxist view. Michael Harrington, *Socialism* (New York: Saturday Review Press, 1972) reinterprets Marx and presents the case for democratic socialism. Robert L. Heilbroner, *Between Capitalism and Socialism* (New York: Random House, 1963) examines the pros and cons of welfare capitalism. For a socialist analysis of the effects of capitalism on the work process see Harry Braverman, *Labor and Monopoly Capital: The Degradation of Work in the Twentieth Century* (New York: Monthly Review Press, 1974).

Democracy. In addition to *On Liberty* Mill's views on democracy are found in *Representative Government.* Thomas Jefferson's principal statements on government have been gathered together in the anthology by Edward Dumbauld, *Political Writings of Thomas Jefferson* (Indianapolis, Indiana: Bobbs-Merrill, 1957). S. I. Benn and R. S. Peters, *Principles of Political Thought* (New York: Free Press, 1965), relates democratic theory to larger questions of social policy. For a highly readable study of the various contemporary meanings of "democracy" see C. B. Macpherson, *The Real World of Democracy* (New York: Oxford University Press, 1966). Henry B. Mayo, *Democratic Theory* (New York: Oxford University Press) is a scholarly, contemporary defense of democracy that combines elements from both liberal democratic theory and democratic pluralism. A. De Grazia, *Public and Republic* (New York: Alfred A. Knopf, 1951) deals especially with the American democratic tradition. For criticism of democracy see Plato's *The Republic* and Hitler's *Mein Kampf.* V. I. Lenin, *State and Revolution,* first published in 1918, is commonly regarded as the clearest statement and elaboration of the traditional Marxist view of the state. A joint declaration of the Communist parties of France and Italy in November 1975 states their official commitment to a democratic transition to socialism. The text along with related materials is available in *Socialist Revolution,* No. 29 (Vol. 6, No. 3), July–September 1976. Carl Cohen, ed., *Communism, Fascism, and Democracy* (New York: Random House, 1966) contains a broad selection of readings.

CHAPTER FOUR
Good Character

The concept of good moral character received a fair amount of attention in classical and medieval philosophy. Aristotle's analysis in the *Nichomachean Ethics* of many virtues as a "golden mean" between vicious extremes—for example, courage as a mean between recklessness and cowardice—is still often cited. Most of the views on good character from this period, however, strike us today as outmoded.

During the modern period, questions relating to good character have been generally neglected, although Kant is famous for equating good character almost exclusively with the sense of duty, while a number of British philosophers such as Hume and Mill often came close to equating good character with altruism. Until recently psychologists and educators also tended to neglect these questions with the notable exception of Jean Piaget, whose *The Moral Judgment of the Child* (London: Kegan Paul) was first published in English in 1932. Since 1960, especially in the United States, however, interest in moral development and education has grown rapidly. Thomas Lickona, ed., *Moral Development and Behavior: Theory, Research, and Social Issues* (New York: Holt, Rinehart and Winston, 1976) gives a good idea of the range of interests and the conflicting positions on these issues among psychologists and educators. Philosophers have still not attempted to do much in this area.

CHAPTER FIVE
Religion and Morality

For generally favorable accounts of religion's influence on morality, see A. Campbell Garnett, *Religion and the Moral Life* (New York: Ronald Press, 1933); C. S. Lewis, *Mere Christianity* (New York: Macmillan, 1960); and Hastings Rashdall, *Philosophy and Religion* (London: Gerald Duckworth and Company, 1909).

For critical accounts of religion's effect on morality see Bertrand Russell, *Why I Am Not a Christian* (New York: Simon and Schuster, 1962); John Dewey, *A Common Faith* (New Haven: Yale University Press, 1934); Friedrich Nietzsche, *Beyond Good and Evil* (New York: Random House, 1966); Sigmund Freud, *The Future of an Illusion* (New York: Liveright, 1961); and Erich Fromm, *Psychoanalysis and Religion* (London: Victor Gollancz, 1951). For Marxist views on religion see Part Six, "Religion," in Howard Selsam and Harry Martel, eds., *Reader in Marxist Philosophy* (New York: International Publishers, 1963).

Ian Ramsey, ed., *Christian Ethics and Contemporary Philosophy* (New York: Macmillan, 1966) presents a variety of views. Sören Kierkegaard, *Fear and Trembling* (London: Oxford University Press, 1946) is a now classic attempt to understand the moral implications of the Biblical story of Abraham and Isaac.

On mysticism see W. T. Stace, *Mysticism and Philosophy* (Philadelphia: J. P. Lippincott, 1960) and F. C. Happold, *Mysticism* (Baltimore: Penguin, 1963). William James, *Varieties of Religious Experience* (New York: Mentor, 1958) also contains much of interest on mysticism. See also David Solomon, ed., *LSD: The Consciousness Expanding Drug* (New York: Putnam, 1966).

For a modern version of the theological principle see Emil Brunner, *The Divine Imperative* (Philadelphia: Westminster, 1947).

CHAPTER SIX
Right Conduct

A classic statement of moral relativism is found in Edward H. Westermarck, *Ethical Relativity* (New York: Harcourt, Brace, and World, 1932). Ruth Benedict, *Patterns of Culture* (Boston: Houghton Mifflin, 1934) shows the wide range of social organizations and moral orientations to be found among different peoples. For a strong criticism of moral relativism see Walter Stace, *The Concept of Morals* (New York: Macmillan, 1965).

The fullest and best-known statement of the emotivist view is found in Charles Stevenson, *Ethics and Language* (New Haven: Yale University Press, 1944). Shorter versions are found in Chapter Six of Alfred Jules Ayer, *Language, Truth and Logic* (New York: Dover, 1946) and in Charles Stevenson, "The Emotive Meaning of Ethical Terms," *Mind,* Vol. xlvi (1937).

The classic statement of utilitarianism is J. S. Mill, *Utilitarianism.* Henry Sidgwick, *Methods of Ethics* (London: Cambridge University Press, 1874) is the major work of a later nineteenth-century utilitarian whom many philosophers rank with Mill. For a criticism of the utilitarian view of distributive justice see the readings by John Rawls and Robert Nozick listed for Chapter Three, page 185. An interesting exchange regarding act utilitarianism versus rule utilitarianism is found in J. J. C. Smart and Bernard Williams, *Utilitarianism: For and*

Against (New York: Cambridge University Press, 1973). See also John Rawls, "Two Concepts of Rules," *Philosophical Review,* Vol. 64 (1955), pp. 3–32.

On punitive justice and related questions there are two excellent anthologies: Bernard Berofsky, ed., *Free Will and Determinism* (New York: Harper and Row, 1966) and Sidney Morgenbesser and James Walsh, *Free Will* (Englewood Cliffs, New Jersey: Prentice-Hall, 1962).

INDEX

A

Abilities
  happiness as realization of, 16–17
  as measure of merit, 40–42
Accommodation, as defined by Dewey, 20, 24, 139–140
Achievement, as measure of merit, 40–42
Act utilitarianism, 159–163
Adaptability, of human species, 27–29
Adaptation, as defined by Dewey, 20, 139–140
Adjustment, as defined by Dewey, 20, 139–140
Adler, Mortimer J. (1902–   ), 183
Afterlife, *see* Immortality
Aggression
  and the development of conscience according to Freud,
    103
  intraspecies aggression among human beings, 32
Alienation, from the product of one's labor according to Marx,
    71–72
Allende Gossens, Salvador (1908–1973), 89
Altruism, *see* Benevolence
Anomie, 144
Anselm, Saint (1033–1109), 137
Anthropomorphism, 13
Aquinas, Saint Thomas (1225–1274), 137, 138, 183
  happiness as a life in conformity to nature, 11–15
  on labor theory of value, 43–44
  on reason and faith, 138
"Aristocracy of virtue and talent," 86
Aristotle (384–322 B.C.), 18, 183, 186–187
  happiness as a life in conformity to nature, 11–15
Artificial, as opposed to natural, 11–12
Asceticism, 126, 134–136
Association, freedom of, 58

D

L

M

N

O

P

About the Author

Robert G. Olson began his study of philosophy as an undergraduate at the University of Minnesota and continued his studies at Columbia University, the Sorbonne in Paris, and the University of Michigan. He became a doctor of the Sorbonne in 1953 and was awarded the American Ph.D. by the University of Michigan in 1957.

He has published regularly in the philosophical journals since early in his career, especially in the area of ethics. *Ethics: A Short Introduction* is his fifth book. The earlier books were *An Introduction to Existentialism, The Morality of Self-Interest, A Short Introduction to Philosophy,* and *Meaning and Argument*.

Professor Olson taught at Columbia from 1958 to 1961 and at Rutgers from 1961 to 1969. In 1969 he accepted the chairmanship of the Department of Philosophy at The Brooklyn Center of Long Island University.